LAME BRAIN

My Journey Back to Real Life

Rick Roberts

Mount James Publishing

Lame Brain by Rick Roberts, copyright © 2015 by Rick Roberts.
Copyright © 2015 by Mount James Publishing.
Song lyrics from "Once is all You Need" written by Rick Roberts, copyright © 1982 by Warner Tamerlane/El Sueno Music, BMI)
Prologue by David Luce, M.D., copyright © 2015 by David Luce, M.D., printed by permission of David Luce, M.D.
Epilogue by Mary Roberts, copyright © 2015 by Mary Roberts, printed by permission of Mary Roberts.

This book is based on true events about the life of singer/songwriter Rick Roberts. All rights reserved. In accordance with the U.S. Copyright Act of 1976, no part of this publication may be reproduced, distributed, or transmitted in any form or by any means, or stored in a database or retrieval system, without prior written permission of the publisher, Mount James Publishing.

Edited by Written Dreams/Brittiany Koren and Cynthia Brackett-Vincent
Cover art design and layout by ENC Graphic Services/Ed Vincent
Cover Cartoon Illustration by Steve Wesley; Spotlight © Ramcreativ/Shutterstock.com;
Question Marks © art4all/Shutterstock.com; Musical Notes © Padalnitski/Shutterstock.com

ISBN-13: 978-0-9964144-2-5

Category: Biography/True Life Memoir, Non-Fiction

First Print Edition November 2015

Printed in the United States of America.
0 1 2 3 4 5 6 7 8 9 0

Books
Song Stories and Other Left-Handed Recollections

Albums
Flying Burrito Brothers (self-titled)
The Last of the Red Hot Burritos
Firefall (self-titled)
Luna Sea
Élan
Undertow
Clouds Across the Sun

Solo Albums
Windmills
She Is the Song

*Footnote: Roberts-Meisner Band never recorded any albums, but played as far as East as Atlantic City to Honolulu and the 20th Anniversary Salute of the Byrds played from Seattle to New York, the four corners of the U.S., both bands of which Rick Roberts was a member.

Preface

By W. David Luce, M.D.

The first time I met Rick Roberts was in my office when he came to me looking for a primary care physician. It was noteworthy only because I had never had anyone in my practice whose job description was "Songwriter."

"Songwriter?" I asked.

"Songwriter," he said and nodded in reply.

"Do I know anything that you might have written?" I asked.

"You may know this one," he said as he sang the opening lines from "You Are the Woman". And indeed, I did know that song, and many of his others.

My musical generation was The Beatles and The Rolling Stones, but I surely had heard the music of Rick Roberts and Firefall. However, as I began to know Rick as his physician, it was his ongoing relationship with alcohol that dominated the scene. This intelligent, engaging rock star was absolutely doing his best to kill himself.

The list of ailments that played themselves out in Rick's body is formidable: alcohol addiction, cerebellar atrophy, pulmonary emboli, cirrhosis, hepatic encephalopathy, and traumatic brain injury to name the major players. That he survived all of these health crises (any one of them could/should have killed him) is amazing and miraculous.

Rick Roberts' life is a story of two devotions. The first was his total devotion to alcohol for so many years. This was a devotion that knew no limits. Indeed, Rick continued his affair/marriage to alcohol despite all the obstacles that the legal system could put in his way. He would come into the office and we would know within five seconds that he was still drinking alcohol by his speech and his wobbly, wide-based gait.

The second, and much more profound devotion, was the devotion that Mary Roberts demonstrated for Rick. It is my professional and personal opinion that Mary just refused to let Rick kill himself. Through her love and total devotion, she made it her full-time job to literally MAKE him stick around. I distinctly remember her bringing Rick to see me when he could not walk or talk, and was in the rear of a station wagon smiling at me as I examined him.* Thank you, Mary!

And then one day, for no obvious reason, Rick divorced alcohol. It has been clinically obvious as he has continued to manifest increased health and mental and motor skills. He is once again the same artistic, creative artist that we all learned to love.

With Rick's recovery, Mary has been out of her job as a caregiver for a number of years now!

***Author's Note:** I think Doctor Luce is being quite modest in his presentation of this situation, but I would also like to add a word of explanation. The station wagon (it was a Chevy Blazer) event took place shortly after my injury had occurred. His office is upstairs in a historic building and has no elevator. I was unable to negotiate the stairs in my wheelchair. I was smiling because he had been kind enough to make a house call (or car call, actually) for me, not because I was loaded. I made a point of never going to his office drunk. Hung over? Probably. But if my speech wasn't terribly clear, that may be because I had not yet started my speech therapy.

Foreword

There is more than one way to become a lame brain. I have personally explored at least two. One of my expeditions into Lame Land was the result of an injury, but the other was nothing more than self-engineered slow-motion suicide. The two elements came together during my recovery from the first so I think I should talk about both as I tell my story. What I hope to describe is my journey through both situations, and how I managed to arrange a trip back into the real world.

Sometimes You Feel Like a Nut…

Chapter One

I'd take immediate issue with anyone who tried to claim I was accident prone, but having had a fairly adventurous nature as a kid, I definitely got into my share of scrapes. After reaching my alleged adulthood, I've still had a number of untoward incidents take place as I went about my day-to-day business. But considering the fact that I was never much of a sit around guy, it's my opinion that a certain amount of reversals are nothing more than the natural course of events. Although I will admit a few of them were a trifle unusual. Or just really dumb.

* * *

Over the course of my life, I've cracked my head open a number of times, each with varying consequences. The very first time was when I was all of five years old. I was enrolled in kindergarten, and back in those days it wasn't anything like what I'm told preschool is like today. In 1955, all we did was gather for a group baby-sitting session. They read us little kid stories, we brought a lunch, and we all ate together. We finger-painted and had arts and crafts (of a very rudimentary sort), we had nap time, and prolonged play periods.

In theory, it was mainly a chance for little boys and girls to get used to interacting with one another. In practice, most of the little boys hung out together and most of the little girls did the same. I, however, had already started to develop what would be a driving consideration during much of my life. I liked girls. *A lot!*

I don't mean I wanted to play girl games or anything like that. But I had already discovered that girls could be very attractive.

One morning at our first play period, I spotted Nancy Wilson, the prettiest girl in the class. She was up on the jungle gym, that construction of metal bars specifically designed for kids to climb on. I proceeded to scramble up the bars trying to catch up to her, and also to impress her with my remarkable catlike agility. But since it was morning, there was dew all over the bars and they were very slippery.

Just when I had gotten almost to the top, about eight feet above the ground, my hand slipped on the wet bar I was reaching for and I lost my grip. I plunged all the way to the bottom row of bars no more than a foot from the grass, and hit my head on one of them. I split my left eyebrow open.

Within seconds, members of the school staff were there. They picked me up and carried me inside, where they laid me down on a table.

The adult in charge called my parents and told them what had happened, and got permission to take me to the emergency room. I had to have some stitches in my eyebrow, but I was pretty sure I had impressed Nancy. Or at least I hoped so.

She must not have been *too* impressed though, because the incident didn't stick with her. I spoke to her on the phone about it a couple of years ago, and she couldn't remember anything like that ever happening in kindergarten.

I was disappointed, because the event was my first of many romance-based injuries, and all my class pictures show my scar to prove it.

Head—three stitches.

* * *

Even though it has nothing to do with my head, I should mention I had my first hernia operated on that same year. Hernia operations weren't quite as advanced in the mid '50s as they were when I had my next one—twenty-three years later. I was given general anesthesia and the whole works. I kept up my courage with visions of the mounds of ice cream I had heard about them giving kids after surgery. After my operation, the doctors couldn't seem to stop the bleeding, so they had to put a surgical clamp on my testicles. All the ice cream in the city wouldn't have compensated me for the pain I don't really think you'd want to hear about. But they didn't give me ice cream. They said that was for kids who had just had their tonsils out. I've still got my tonsils, sixty years later.

I did come dangerously close to getting myself ejected from the hospital, though. They kept me for a few days for observation, and on the third day they gave me a wheelchair so I could get around the hospital.

To a five-year-old, anything with wheels is a race car. So that's how I treated it. The morning after they equipped me with my little hot rod, I was barreling down one of the corridors at full speed when they wheeled an elderly man out of his room on a gurney, directly into my way. I hit him broadside, with enough force to dislodge his IV (still glass in those days), which hit and shattered on the hallway floor.

My punishment: the hospital staff took away my wheelchair and confined me to my room. They also said I was ready to go home remarkably soon after that incident. Come to think of it, maybe I *was* ejected.

Hernia—eight stitches.

* * *

My next run-in with injury was my own fault and happened when I was eight. We used to live next door to the Thomas', a very old couple who brought their niece's son to live with them. He was a year older than I was, and rather portly. His mom had named him Holly, for reasons I never knew, and I will admit I teased him occasionally about that. Sometimes, I would make some smart remark and then run away. Not very gentlemanly of me, but what can I say? I was eight.

He was several inches taller than I was too, so I knew if he could ever catch me, he would be able to do me serious bodily harm. But I knew he couldn't run that fast.

At one point he decided to take other measures and shot me in the butt with a BB gun. My parents had heard me tease him, and even though they told his family, they then told me I half-way deserved it. My mother warned me teasing always had a bad result. So I stopped doing it. But that wasn't the event I'm talking about. Evidently, Holly was holding a grudge.

Then one day he caught me by surprise when I was passing his backyard. He put me in a headlock and muscled me into his yard. Then he managed to get my T-shirt over my head and pulled me down to the ground—at which point he sat on me. His old grand uncle was something of a gardener and among his horticultural efforts was a little pepper bush. I'm not sure what kind of peppers they were, but they were red and about an inch long. I had tried to eat one once, but they were way too hot for me.

Holly had collected about a dozen of them in a cup, and he proceeded to rub the peppers all over my skin on my whole upper body, getting the juice all over me. I am talking about some serious pain. The juice raised blisters all over my stomach and chest for two weeks. The couple next door sent Holly back to his mom.

Stomach and chest—no stitches, countless blisters.

* * *

I managed to keep my head and my body injury free for the next few years, but when I hit eleven, I made up for lost time.

My best friend in elementary school was a kid named Donald Dykes. We both lived within a block of our school, on opposite sides, and we were both smart and undersized. We competed with one another in schoolwork and in games, and we were fairly athletic for little guys. We would go over to the school grounds after school was out for the day and on weekends to high-jump, or race, or play two-man dodge ball. (You play two-man dodge ball by using a wall as the backstop. One man throws, and one man dodges. Then the ball bounces off the wall and back to the thrower.)

We played on the asphalt court of our school, and one day while we were playing a game I was the dodger. We were pretty evenly matched, both as throwers and dodgers. The one thing I could never seem to do was to jump high enough to clear the ball when Donald got me to go into the air.

On this occasion, Donald faked, got me to jump, and then he threw. Somehow, unlike the usual outcome, I managed to clear the ball. Unfortunately, I was so excited I forgot to land. I came down hard squarely on my chin, and split it wide open. Immediately, I started to bleed profusely all over the pavement.

Donald lived about two houses over from where we were playing, so we went to his house where I could get a bandage. I figured that would be enough to take care of it.

I was wearing a white T-shirt, and the front was showing quite a bit of red already, so when Donald's mother saw us, it spooked her. She asked me what I wanted to do, and I told her it was no big deal. I wanted to walk home and only needed a Band-Aid. I put the bandage on my chin, and then headed home. Evidently, Mrs. Dykes called my mother, because when I came into my backyard she was standing at the back door waiting for me.

By this time my T-shirt had an upside down "V" of blood from my chin to my waist, and the bandage was nothing but a sagging u-shaped soggy thing clinging to my chin. I never got inside the house. I was hustled right into the car with a thick towel from Mom, and driven straight to the ER.

Chin—three stitches.

* * *

I'm certainly not a one-trick pony when it comes to stupid ways to injure myself.

My family lived about a block from the Gulf of Mexico, but it was several miles over the causeway to get to Clearwater Beach—a place that was a lot better for swimming than the channel between the mainland and the islands.

On the other hand, we were also just a block down the street from The Fort Harrison Hotel which wouldn't become the headquarters of Scientology until a couple of decades later. They had a great pool, and it was easy to buy a club membership, allowing the member full access to swim there. They also had a diving coach who gave lessons, and a swim club.

I asked the diving coach to teach me how to do several of the more difficult dives (for a twelve-year-old), but the most impressive and the hardest one was a gainer, or full gainer. I don't know if it's still called that, but it's the dive where

Lame Brain

you go off the board forwards, and then do a back flip in the air into the water.

I mastered the dive under the coach's watchful eye and performed it maybe two times when no one was around. When the weekend came and there were a bunch of people at the pool, including my mom and dad, I decided it would be the perfect time to show off my new trick. I called for my parents to watch me, and naturally, that got the attention of everyone at the pool. I did my masterful approach and executed my dive.

Then, as was my normal routine, I went to the bottom of the pool, touched the drain, and swam underwater to the ladder. I surfaced, and looked around to get the approval of my "audience", but there was no one looking at me. They were all staring down at the water.

When I turned around to look, I saw two things. There were several swimmers down at the bottom of the pool, and there was a long thin line of blood tracing a line from directly below the diving board to the bottom, and then over to the ladder where I was treading water. It was only then I noticed that my head hurt.

What I learned later was that I had clipped the back of my head on the board when I did my flip, and when I went straight to the bottom, everyone thought I'd knocked myself unconscious. My father, the lifeguard, and several other men immediately dived in to pull me out. They were the swimmers I saw at the bottom of the pool. I was disappointed because absolutely no one complimented me on the dive, and minus the blood, I thought I had executed it well.

Head—two stitches.

* * *

Down in Florida, since we never saw snow, we substituted rock fights for snowball fights. Nothing serious—no rocks bigger than shooter marbles were allowed. One day after a good rain we were having a pretty good rock ball fight (sometimes, if it had rained, we covered the rocks with mud…hence, rock balls. Don't ask me why we didn't just call them mud balls. Oh wait. Mud balls don't have rocks in them), and I stood up from behind our fort wall a little too high. As I looked down to make another rock ball, I got clocked right on top of my head. It didn't knock me out, but it did split my head and bleed a lot. That led to another visit to the emergency room, where by now I was getting to be on a first name basis with everyone.

Head—two stitches.

* * *

The other hernia operation at the age of twenty-eight is hardly worth mentioning. They only used local anesthetic and I joked with the nurses throughout the procedure. Until, that is, the doctor told me to clam up because the nurses were laughing too much to do their job. I left the hospital the same afternoon.

Actually, that part is worth mentioning.

Before the operation, I asked the doctor how long most patients stayed in the hospital following the procedure. He told me some people left the same afternoon or the next day at the latest. Since I wanted to be a real manly man, I called my lady friend and left (in quite a lot of pain) that afternoon.

When I talked to the doctor two days later at a check-up, he asked me where I had disappeared to. I told him I had gone home. I said I was just following his description of the general behavior of most patients. He said, "Are you crazy? I was just saying that to inspire you. Nobody leaves three hours after their surgery!"

I probably would have felt stupid, but I was too busy feeling the pain.

Hernia—three stitches.

* * *

I've also had a few interesting experiences that involved automobiles, if you find potentially fatal car accidents interesting. Luckily, with one exception, I managed to survive the car episodes without any *serious* damage to myself, although most of the cars didn't fare as well.

* * *

After spending most of my adult life as a recording artist, I ran into a bit of an unforeseen obstacle in the early 1980s. When I left Firefall and moved from Colorado to California in 1981, I was suddenly confronted with some legal matters that stopped me from pursuing my musical interests for a while. Once I managed to get most of them worked out, I decided it was time for me to go out and start gigging again.

I did a tour as a solo opening act for a headlining David Crosby and his band, coupled with a solo Roger McGuinn as a second act, and a duo tour with Chris Hillman a few months later. Aside from that, I hadn't been working much. Just when it looked like I was facing more time off, I got booked for another short trip. I was going to be gone for about three days, and then be home for a while.

I had a really nice Mercedes 450SL back then. When it came time to head out on the road, I drove it down to LAX (Los Angeles International Airport) from my house in Malibu Lake, and parked in the secured area.

It was January, but the weather was really nice. I had my rag top on the car, so I closed it and locked everything up. I was looking forward to the shows and I was excited about getting out to play again.

When I came back three days later, someone had managed to cut open the top, get in and completely remove my stereo system. In the process, they also screwed up the ignition wiring so the car wouldn't start. Considering how easily the thieves were able to get into the secure parking area, I was amazed at how complex a process it was to get a tow truck there. I was without any wheels for two weeks.

By the time I got my car back from the repair shop it was early February, but the weather was still very warm. I picked it up, and drove back out to Malibu. I had dinner at Alice's Restaurant, where I met Morgan Fairchild, who looked even more beautiful in person than she did on TV. That definitely put me in a good mood, and since it was such a nice night, I decided to put down the top and take a nice drive along the Mulholland Highway before I went home. Most of that road is filled with curves, but there is one stretch south of Malibu Canyon Road (Las Virgenes Road) that is straight for about a mile. Then it takes a big S curve and goes back to snaking along the crest of the Santa Monica Mountains.

I turned onto the road, and punched the gas pedal. As I came to the beginning of the big S, I realized I was driving too fast. I braked a little and negotiated the curve, but when I came to the second part of the S curve I was still going too fast. No big deal. I started to brake again.

At just that moment, I hit a patch of loose gravel on the pavement and immediately went 90 degrees sideways. The car hit and fractured a big power pole, and snapped the electric lines. I was not wearing a seat belt, and was catapulted about 100 feet out of the car.

I hit the ground just below my neck with my shoulders taking the brunt of the impact and walked away from the scene. But the car rolled over a couple of times as it went down the side of the hill only to have the 50,000-volt power lines land directly in the car cab! If I'd been wearing my seatbelt, I might or might not have survived the rollover, but if I had, I'd have been fried meat when the power lines landed!

I later found out that I'd suffered shin splints in both my legs, probably from hitting them on the steering wheel as I made my exit from the car. At the time, I was in shock and didn't feel a thing. And I recently found that somewhere during the accident two of the vertebras in my neck got fused. I'm betting it happened when I landed that night. Needless to say, that was the end of my Mercedes. Despite the loss of the car, I was very lucky that night.

Neck—no stitches, but two fused vertebra.

* * *

After I totaled my Mercedes, I went back to Colorado and drove my other car, a BMW 530i, back out to California to take the Merc's place. Originally I had

---

*Post Script: About two years ago I suddenly felt a scratchy spot on my forehead one day. It was my last glass chip. It had decided to make an exit after being imbedded up there for nearly thirty years. It came out the next night while I was sleeping and I never found it.

left it in Boulder because somewhere deep inside I figured I would be coming back one day.

In the spring of 1987, I had come back from another musical road trip, and on my way from the airport I stopped to see a friend in the hospital. I visited for an hour or two, and then headed home. I had moved several times since Malibu Lake, and was now living about a block from the water in Manhattan Beach. I always took the Pacific Coast Highway home from the airport, and since the hospital was in Santa Monica, I took the same route from there.

It was about 9:00 in the evening and traffic was fairly light. I had always read that, especially at night, it's a good idea to glance away from the white lines occasionally to avoid hypnotizing yourself while you drive so I made it an regular practice to do so.

Just north of Manhattan Beach there is an oil refinery next to the highway and usually a couple of oil tankers are off shore taking on cargo through the underwater pipes. On this particular evening, there were three.

I was rolling along in the Beamer at about 55 miles per hour when I took a brief glance at the tankers all lit up out on the water. When I returned my eyes to the road, the car in front of me had stopped dead in my lane. I slammed on my brakes, turned my wheel as far as I could to the left, and managed to avoid hitting it.

Unfortunately, my car then turned a full 180 degrees, skidded across four lanes of highway (luckily unoccupied), and crashed through a steel pole two inches in diameter that was part of the refinery fence. The car finally came to rest about four feet from an uncovered pool of acid used in the refining process.

I shattered the windshield with my head, and the car was totaled. I never found out why the guy in front of me had stopped because he drove away, oblivious to what was happening right behind him. Other people driving by did stop, and by the greatest good fortune, one of them was a doctor. Maybe "good fortune" does not do proper justice to the situation. God was looking out for me that night. I had no auto insurance at the time, and I think I must have been in shock, too. I was telling the onlookers I was okay, but I could use a ride home.

The doctor said I needed to go to a hospital. I told him I wasn't insured so that wouldn't work. Having just come back from my little tour, I had a couple of thousand dollars on me. Now, I know that doesn't sound too bright, but I had been paid in cash for my show the night before. I hadn't had a chance to get to a bank on the road, so all the cash was still in my pocket. I pulled out a wad of money and offered to pay him if he could help me with some immediate care. He asked me what I was doing with so much cash, and I told him who I was and why I had the dough.

Against seemingly impossible odds, he knew of me and my music, and said he would help me. He took me back to his office in Marina Del Rey, the huge boat marina with a little town attached, which was just up the road. He spent most of the night picking tiny pieces of glass out of my face, and then stitching me up. He also took a bunch of photos which he showed me later. There was a silver-dollar sized section of my skull showing, and the rest of my face was doing a pretty fair imitation of a pound of ground beef.

It took an amazing number of stitches to piece my face back together, and I referred to myself as "Rickenstein" for about a month. I'm embarrassed to admit I cannot remember the good doctor's name. I was happy to pay him a fairly large sum of money, but there is no price I can put on how grateful I am to him to this day for his kind attentions.

The whole episode took place with no police on the scene, even though they evidently did show up after the doctor and I had left. I know this because they towed my car to the pound. I didn't see it until about a week later, and when I did, I was astonished that, aside from my face, I walked away from yet another potentially fatal accident.

The mainframe of the car was so bent out of shape that the car was only resting on three wheels at a time. A back one on one side, a front one on the other, and an optional third one. You could tip it back and forth between the two wheels in the air with one finger to ground one, but you could never get all four wheels on the ground at once.

I admit, I started to tremble when I saw how completely I had destroyed it. I'm sure I still have one little piece of glass in my forehead—just to serve as a reminder. Actually, this was more a face injury than a head injury. The only common ground was that it was possible to see my skull. The one thing I will say about it is really just a perverse point of pride—that incident is the big kahuna of stitch counts.

Face—a whopping one hundred and sixty-eight stitches.

* * *

Some of my experiences with automobiles have been unique, especially in comparison to the experiences I've heard from other people who've been in accidents. I would bet money on the fact that not too many people can truthfully say they have actually run over *themselves*. I have. I'm not talking about forgetting to put on the parking brake and having your car bump into you. I mean having a hand on the wheel, and literally running over myself. Hard to believe? Yes. But definitely possible. Here's how I did it.

In 1989, I rejoined the then current lineup of Firefall for about three years. Sometime during that period, we did a show in Branson, Missouri back in the days before it was easy to fly in there. It was mid-summer, and predictably hot and humid. The band had driven down from St. Louis, which is a 250-mile trip, and by the time we got into town we were all ready to go relax in our hotel rooms before going over to the outdoor venue for our sound check.

When we got to the hotel, there was a line of about five or six people waiting to check in ahead of us. It took us nearly a half hour to get to the desk and receive our room keys, and none of us were in the best of moods. When I had got my key, I stomped outside to retrieve my suitcase. The rental car with my bag in the trunk was parked in the driveway in front of the hotel which was on a little hill. The ignition was still running, so I assumed the car was in park.

Something I didn't know about an automatic transmission is that when the car is facing uphill, it can still be in drive, and the fact that the engine is engaged will act like a brake to keep it from rolling back down the hill. But when you turn off the ignition... Well, that's when the situation changes. The drive position effectively becomes the same as neutral.

I opened the door, reached in, and turned off the engine to grab the keys. That's when I found out the car was in *drive* instead of park. As it started to roll backwards, I looked down the hill and saw there was another car sitting at the bottom of the hill about forty feet away with two little girls on the front seat.

Try and visualize this: I started from a standing position next to the car, but I immediately used my right hand, with the keys, to grab the steering wheel. Meanwhile, I was supporting myself on the moving car with my left hand wrapped around the open window of the door. I had my right foot in the car, desperately trying to reach the brake pedal, and my left leg dragging along on the ground under the car.

Needless to say, my steering was something less than wonderful. The car was veering erratically across the driveway. Since the lobby was on the crest of the hill, and the sidewalk outside the front was level, a little wall had been built that got higher in comparison to the driveway as you moved away from the lobby door.

Once again, God and good fortune were smiling on me, because three things happened at the same time. First, the car swerved right up against the wall. Second, at just that point in the wall, they had put in a one-step stairway for people to get from the driveway up to the sidewalk. And third, I lost my grip, and the car went over my left leg. My upper body went up on to the sidewalk, and my leg was protected from being mashed against the wall, and from the weight of the car by getting into the recessed area of the stairway as the car slammed up against the curb.

This all took place in a matter of about ten seconds, although to me it seemed like ten hours. The bass player drove me to the emergency room, but ultimately the only thing injured, besides my pride, was a severe case of road rash on my left leg and some swelling from the limited amount of weight of the car wheel my leg bore. I ended up doing the show that night, but I had to perform in our drummer's sweat pants because the swelling in my leg had increased big time so I couldn't get my own pants on. I should mention that the drummer was an inch or two taller, but outweighed me by at least 100 pounds. It took a few

Lame Brain

weeks for my leg to get back to normal, but the car I was "driving" managed to miss the car at the bottom of the hill, and the two little girls were safe.

No stiches, just swelling.

* * *

Well that just about covers my medical history, at least in terms of accidents. I have incurred one other significant head injury in my life, but I don't think this is the place where I should describe that one. I've said that the numerous times in my life when I opened my skull have had varying consequences, and it's true. But all of these I've spoken of so far have been either whimsical childhood scrapes or events that were easy to discount. My last injury was no laughing matter. It literally changed my life.

Brain Salad

Chapter Two

I've told you about all the different ways I managed to bang myself up, and you probably noticed there were a variety of head injuries included. I ended the last chapter by saying there had been one further incident, and there was. But as I also said, it was neither a funny one nor a lesson-learning experience.

At the time it happened, it seemed to be no big thing and much less serious than a number of injuries I had suffered in the past. Just a little household mishap. Apparently, something like 90% of all accidents happen in the home, but I think they're usually more along the lines of mishaps like cutting your finger when you're slicing onions and so forth.

My own accident turned out to be a life-changing occurrence.

A little later, I'll be telling you about the first experience I had in Lame Land, which was a journey fueled by alcohol. In 2006 I was still drinking, but on this occasion, I hadn't had a drop. That's one of the other things that made it so unexpected.

My wife Mary and I had two dogs, both little more than puppies at the time. As puppies are known to do, they loved to chew on things, including ink pens. Sometime around the end of April, one of them had gotten hold of a ballpoint and chewed through it, emptying the ink on our carpet.

We were unable to get the stain out by ourselves, and made an appointment with a cleaning service for a full carpet shampoo. In the meantime, we put down a throw rug to cover the spots. At the time, that seemed like the logical thing to do. It didn't seem like the rug was an object to be feared. But it wasn't long to find out we were mistaken.

One morning about a week before Mother's Day, I managed to get my feet tangled up in the rug and tripped, hitting the left side of my forehead on the corner of our kitchen island. I punched a small hole in my head, but it only bled for about ten minutes before it stopped. As many times as I've whacked my head in my life, I thought nothing more about it. Of course, in hindsight, I have a much clearer picture of things, and I can tell you now that May 6, 2006 is a

Lame Brain

date I won't ever forget.

Mary was at work at the time, and I don't think I even mentioned it to her when she called to check in that day. Since she's a very observant person though, she quickly noticed the puncture wound when she came home that day and asked me what had happened. I told her, but assured her it was nothing to be concerned about.

As the week went by, I started to develop a small blood blister on my forehead. It still didn't strike either of us as anything we should pay any attention to or worry about. Then on Mother's Day, Mary and I were sitting across from one another in our living room when the blister suddenly burst, sending a small spray of blood about four feet into space.

I didn't even feel it, but Mary saw it and told me what had just happened. When I put my fingers to my forehead, they came away with blood on them. I was taking a blood thinner at that time, due to having had a clot in my leg a few years earlier, I thought it would be a good idea to lie down on the hallway floor and let gravity do its work. No sense taking any chances.

Mary wanted me to go to the hospital immediately, because I kept bleeding. I laid a bath towel across my forehead, and said again that it was nothing, and that the bleeding would stop soon.

After an hour, during which I had completely soaked the bath towel with my blood, Mary was getting very insistent about going to the ER. I continued to balk at that choice of action. I know I was being childish, in the same way that guys often do, because like a lot of guys, I hate to go anywhere near a hospital.

The bleeding continued for another three hours and two more full-sized bath towels later before finally my wife laid it on the line for me. Either I got up right then and went to the ER, or she was going to call the paramedics and have me taken in whether I liked it or not. She called it my "two minute warning".

All right, I would go, I told her, but she would see. It was *nothing*. Chances are she saved my life that day, because I still believed the bleeding was almost ready to stop and I probably would have stayed there stretched out on the floor till I bled out.

So I got myself up, and with the towel still clutched to my forehead, made my way slowly down to the car. She drove, and was calm the whole ride there.

When we got to the ER, they put an astringent on the hole in my head and got the bleeding to stop. The nurse asked what had happened. I explained it to her, complete with the description of the four-hour, three bath towel situation. Her next question was how long had I been unconscious. I told her I hadn't been unconscious at all, and she got a very puzzled look on her face.

Then she said, "You should have been."

The on-duty doctor did an EEG, and then they told Mary and I to sit tight while they got a look at what was happening. It took about another hour for the results to be deciphered and the doctor to come back. He briefly informed me about the nature of my injury. I had been mistaken. It hadn't been *nothing*. In fact, it was very definitely *something*.

I had suffered a subdural hematoma and a cranial bleed. In simpler terms, a brain hemorrhage. The doctor left for a little while to give Mary and me a chance to absorb the information. After we had been given sufficient time to come to terms with things, he came back to explain to me how my situation was going to develop. He told me I would lose my ability to walk. He also said that it didn't necessarily have to be a permanent condition. If I was willing to work hard and undergo extensive physical therapy, then and only then, there was a chance that *maybe* I could regain the use of my legs.

"*What?!*" I said, rather stridently. "That can't be right. I hit my head last week, and I'm still walking fine. That's gotta be wrong!" Meanwhile, I was thinking, *What kind of doctor was this guy?*

He understood my doubts, but he told me, "Nonetheless, very shortly you will find yourself no longer able to walk."

I left the hospital with a mixture of feelings, ranging from disbelief to mild anxiety. I decided that I was just going to have to wait and see. For the time being, I intended to go about my business and not worry about something that hadn't happened yet.

* * *

For about a month, everything went along like normal, and I felt pretty sure that my Mother's Day experience was nothing more than a really bad day. Having had numerous encounters with overprotective doctors who were rather alarmist in their dire predictions about my medical future, I thought this was looking suspiciously like another one of those episodes.

Then one morning I rolled out of bed like any other day, with the intention of taking my usual early morning whiz. Only on this day, my legs buckled under me. I collapsed on the carpet and couldn't get up.

"*What's going on?*" I asked myself aloud.

I tried not to panic, but I was very scared. Even though I remembered what the doctor had said, I couldn't accept the fact that his prediction was actually coming to pass. All sorts of things went through my head, such as that I would be okay after a few minutes, or that maybe it was all just psychosomatic; my own imagination causing the situation.

In light of the circumstances I know my reaction was ridiculous, but what it really boiled down to was that I couldn't make myself believe what *seemed* to be happening could possibly *be happening*. I laid there on the floor for a couple of minutes trying to exert my willpower on the situation, to command myself to get up and shake it off. *No go.*

I called out to Mary, who was already up and out in the kitchen, and was used to my regular sunrise pit stop. She came in, and I explained to her what was going on.

Mary asked if we should call a doctor or the paramedics. I told her that wouldn't help anything, and reminded her what the ER physician had said. In my head though, I was still convinced the whole thing was going to pass in a little while. The unreality of having this kind of delayed reaction simply didn't make any sense to me. If I was going to lose my mobility, it would have happened way before this, or so it seemed. *Why would it take a month? And why not suddenly?*

After about an hour, it became clear this was how it was going to be, at least for a little while, so I moved myself from the bedroom to the living room by crawling on my hands and knees. I could still do that, which only reinforced the notion that this would all go away. After all, I could still crawl, so how serious could it really be? The reality of the situation was that I still had most of the muscle control in the rest of my body, but I simply had lost enough of said muscle control or strength in my legs that they wouldn't support my weight. That was another thing that was very confusing. *Why my legs and nothing else?*

For the first week or so, my hands and knees were my only means of transport around the house. My routine was simple. Get out of bed in the morning, crawl to the living room, get up on to the couch (which was done totally with arm leverage) and stay there all day watching TV or reading, except when I needed to go to the bathroom. There I did the same thing, only instead of the couch, I was hoisting myself up onto the toilet.

After a couple of days, my knees were getting a little raw, so I switched to scooting along on my butt and kind of arm paddled myself forward. It must have been quite entertaining to watch me get up and down the stairs in our split-level house. Mainly because I used the same approach there as I did to get from my bed to the couch. One step at a time, bouncy-bouncy, relying strictly on my arms and butt. However, entertaining or not, Mary never teased me or made fun of my situation. She was totally supportive from day number one and every day thereafter.

Periodically, I managed to get to the kitchen where I found a person can operate fairly effectively from a sitting position. As long as the refrigerator door handle isn't too high. I also found if I leveraged myself into a standing position and rested all my weight against the counter, I could do the things that I needed to stand up for. My legs still had enough strength to hold me up as long as I had something to support me, but when I tried to totally put my weight on them or take a step, I collapsed in a heap.

Throughout all this I insisted that Mary keep working, telling her I was okay until this got straightened out. Her instinct was to stay home with me until I was back on my feet. That's an awful pun, but she did want to be there until she was sure I was acclimated to my new abilities, or lack thereof. She tried very hard to convince me to get some sort of help.

When I say she wanted me to get help, I'm sure she was thinking of the physical therapy approach, but I just wasn't listening. I was still stuck in the illusion that this would eventually go away and I'd be fine. That it was all just a big misunderstanding with my body.

I now know Mary was terrified by what had happened, but she never let on how she felt. She kept up a brave front around me through it all. And that was vitally important, considering the mental and physical states I was in. I think if I had known how afraid she was, I might have been too shaken to do anything but lay back and panic. I'm not sure I would ever have marshaled up the determination to fight back against my situation, and as it was, it took quite a while to reach the point of being willing to start that battle.

After about ten days with no change, Mary took it upon herself to get me a wheelchair. The main thing that acquisition changed was how I pursued my by now well-established routine of bed to couch to bathroom and back. With the chair, I had to move myself to the bottom of the bed, and then, with the wheelchair facing me, do a 180-degree turn and sit in the chair seat. I did miss a few times before I got the hang of it and landed solidly on my ass on the floor, much to the chagrin of my coccyx.

Within a few days, I had mastered the maneuver and could wheel myself to my favorite couch. Once I had it down, I have to admit it worked better to make that turn from the chair to the couch rather than having to lift myself from the floor with my arm strength. And I definitely didn't miss the butt-scooting process from the bedroom to the living room. Truth be told, my new mode of transport was a lot easier on my posterior.

It was a very strange period of time. The days went by with me just staying in a sort of suspended animation. I didn't register the passage of time, because for me, every day was the same. I hardly left the house; I didn't go anywhere or do anything.

I'll have a lot more to say about this later, but I had quite a well-developed alcohol problem by that point in my life. Being totally immobilized didn't do anything but amplify the habit.

Before I realized it, the days had turned into months and I was getting uncomfortably comfortable with my disability. I guess I was in kind of an ongoing, gentle state of shock or perhaps a total state of denial. I definitely wasn't looking beyond the moment, or grasping the fact that if I didn't change my response to what had happened to me things would go on like this for the rest of my life.

After several months had passed with no improvement, Mary convinced me that I should try physical therapy, like the doctor had suggested to do back on Mother's Day. I was still very reluctant, but nothing was changing. My legs still wouldn't hold me up, and I was beginning to get a funny feeling that's the way things would stay unless I was willing to seek help. I was starting to sense that below my apparent acceptance of my situation, a hidden reserve of frustration at the condition my life had devolved to was steadily building. The only thing I was sure of was that I felt completely helpless, and it was obvious I wasn't going to get any better by myself. So, I agreed to try the physical therapy route.

It wasn't easy for me to change my mindset and face the situation. In many ways, simply refusing to look at the truth was much safer and trauma-free than accepting the fact that I had somehow allowed my injury to isolate me from the rest of the world.

If I were to force myself to open my eyes and honestly look around me, I would have some difficult decisions to make. Did I really have the courage, or for that matter, the desire to put up the fight required to change things?

And even if I was willing to try, what guarantee did I have that I could win the battle? *None!* But Mary and I talked about it, and we both agreed that there was no shortcut available to make things right again. I was either going to have to go on the attack, or surrender to my circumstance and accept life in a wheelchair forever. I decided then and there that was a life I couldn't accept, at least not without a fight.

With no guarantees of success, we took the only other option—the one I had been so determined not to take—and decided it was going to be necessary to find some assistance.

So, we went looking for the right place to get help.

The Long and Winding Road

Chapter Three

Mary and I (as will become apparent, she and I were in this fight together) looked around the area with the intention of identifying the kind of facility we'd need to enroll me in. Would a hospital out-patient situation be best, or a place specializing in physical therapy, or maybe even a private trainer/therapist who could treat me at home?

Now that I had enlisted myself in the campaign, *or thought I had*, it was important to have a game plan. I made the mistake of letting a few of my friends know I was intending to make a full scale effort to regain the use of my legs, and it created an avalanche of unexpected and unnecessary advice.

I was bombarded with suggestions from people who had very little first-hand knowledge of what I would need to successfully challenge my body. I'm sure they all meant well, but their input was not really of much use in choosing a place to battle out my fight.

In the end, we did what we should have done to begin with when I first lost the use of my legs. We went back to the hospital where they had originally diagnosed my condition and asked them to provide us with some possible places that might offer what I needed. They provided us with several, and told us we should do our own research to make up our own minds about which we thought would work best for me.

Our first choice was Craig Hospital in Denver, one of the most respected facilities in the country for brain injury rehabilitation, but I didn't have medical insurance at the time and the only way they would accept me was if I put down a $10,000 deposit. That took them off the list.

Then we contacted Boulder Community Hospital. I initially agreed to start my therapy there. Their rates were a whole lot more reasonable and they were willing to let me work out a payment plan.

We did go to the hospital, and I even persevered through an intake interview with one of the therapists, but that's as far as it went. I was put off by a lot of seemingly unimportant questions and other things that I couldn't see as related to what I was trying to accomplish. *Paperwork*.

At least, that's what I told myself. In truth, I didn't have a good reason why I chose not to continue. I think I was just confused and scared and still didn't know what I wanted. I ended up blowing it off, and went back to the imaginary security of my self-imposed but familiar home detention. Even though it may not have been the way to solve my problems, it was safe and undemanding.

About that time, Mary left her most recent position, which was ironically, with an insurance company. She was with me at home for a few weeks until she realized that her being there didn't bring about any change in my condition. She was still my most important support and my main source of strength, but her presence in the house wasn't the primary way to bring that support into play.

There was nothing she could do to help me as long as I wasn't doing anything to help myself. And that wasn't going to happen until I could commit myself in my mind willingly to some sort of therapy. And I wasn't going to commit to *any* kind of therapy until I had a much clearer idea of what was really going on in my life; and more importantly, what was going on in my mind.

Realizing what was happening to me may sound like something any idiot could have seen, but it was not as simple as it sounds. In spite of all the unchallenged physical evidence of the situation, a portion of my brain was struggling to deny the truth. I was still fighting a battle with my own denial.

So Mary went back to work—this time at Service Magic, a division of the Interactive Corporation (IAC)—on the condition that I promised to hire a home care service.

After another few months had slipped away, and some of the bad taste in my mouth about the first time around had faded from my mind, it was time to get truly committed to my recovery. It had been three months since I thought I'd been serious before, but when I was suddenly face-to-face with the magnitude of the task, it was disheartening to say the least.

The false starts that had come with our first efforts had pretty much deflated my initial confidence. There had been too much confusion and too many seemingly irrelevant distractions involved for me to hold on to my resolve. And at the outset, I had never even begun to consider the financial aspects of things. Throughout the process, I couldn't help but feel a sense of hopelessness threaded among the details and form fill-outs that made it all seem like a completely wasted effort.

Mary and I talked it over again. I would give physical therapy another try, and this time I wouldn't be so easily deterred. I went to Longmont United Hospital, and they placed me with a therapist named Julie who was very good. But since my upper body had been doing most of the work for over a year, simple weight considerations made it difficult for me to pursue my recovery with her. She wasn't big enough to physically support my body while I was still in the early stages of the exercise program I needed to undertake.

So I once again bowed out, but not for quite so long this time and without such a bitter taste in my mouth. Gradually my haze of indecision was lifting and my future began to take shape. I started to realize that not only did I need to start my therapeutic road, but the only real chance I had to beat my disability was to attack it. No more *accepting* things as they were. It was time to go on the offensive. Yeah, I know I'd said that before, but there was a difference this time.

First of all, I had weathered the initial barrage of surprises regarding details and distractions, and I wasn't going to be derailed by them again. Secondly, by trial and error, I had explored a number of the things that didn't work, so the available avenues to pursue had shrunk. Thirdly, there was the additional bonus of Mary's newly acquired work insurance coverage, so I could no longer plead the cost as an excuse to delay things. And finally, as I said before, it was clearer than ever that what the original doctor in the ER had told me on Mother's Day over a year ago was completely true. Unless I was willing to commit to time and hard work, then this was the way things would stay permanently. I think I had finally and irrevocably come to terms with that. I was much more prepared than I had been not to let any of the small stuff do me in.

But there was still the matter of connecting with the right therapist. Mary called the hospital and explained the situation—why it hadn't worked well before with a woman. They said they understood and would make the necessary arrangements for a change. This time they assigned me a former gymnast named Helmut Tingstad. We went through the intake interview, and the work began.

By this time, I had been on my back for about sixteen months. Everything in me said that that was not acceptable, so I figured I'd better get on with it. After the interview, we made an appointment for a few days later and I went home to try to build my resolve.

I started off by making an agreement with myself that I was not going to sit in a wheelchair for the rest of my life, and no matter how discouraging things might look at any point, I would stick to my efforts and do my very best to beat this thing. In other words, I promised myself that this time I wouldn't quit. The main thing, though, was not to let myself be thrown off by anything unexpected. That had been my downfall every other time I started therapy—something would come into play that didn't match my scenario and I'd be ready to give up the fight again. It was a matter of flexibility.

I finally got it through my head that I had no way of knowing what the shape of this adventure would be so I had no right to be surprised by anything that happened. It wasn't as if anybody had given me a script for the journey.

You may notice I have spoken of how I 'finally came to terms with' or how I 'began to realize' a number of times as I describe my stuttering entry into my recovery. I don't mean to be redundant, but that's the way it was. Every time I turned around I was confronted with some other new awakening to what was necessary to make this all work. And sad to say, with the condition my head was in, I often came to the same 'new' awareness several times.

This time there really *was* a difference. Every other attempt I had made had begun with a shadow of doubt lingering in the background about whether any of this was going to be worth it in the end. Would *it* make any difference in my condition? Or would I end up just the same as I was when I started this journey except for having wasted a lot of time and money in the empty pursuit of an impossible dream? I wasn't aware of that shadow at the time, but now I knew it had been there by virtue of its absence.

Suddenly I found myself eager for the challenge and unwilling to believe I could wind up any way except triumphant when all was said and done.

* * *

I remember the very first session. It was rather daunting when I started, because Helmut immediately had me get out of my chair and stand with the support of a walker. He asked me to walk as many steps as I could before I felt completely exhausted. Then, he said, I could sit back down in the wheelchair which was being pushed along directly behind me.

I managed four steps before I thought I would fall down if I took another. I looked at Mary, who was standing close by, and saw the tears running down her cheeks. Even if it was only four steps, I had turned a corner and started my road to recovery.

One Small Step for Man…

Chapter Four

From that day on, the next two-and-a-half years of my time and attention were dominated by my therapy. I'd finally given in and accepted it as the only possible path to recovery. Assuming there *would be* a recovery. That didn't require all that much of a sacrifice or change of schedule on my part; there hadn't been much else going on since I stopped walking anyway.

But there was another thing entirely going on with my finances. I didn't really care much at the time. I had more important things to think about after all, but the insurance provided by Mary's work policy wasn't nearly enough to cover the expenses involved for my therapy. As a result, I began to borrow against the royalties on my music.

Broadcast Music Incorporated had a very helpful program set up with U.S. Bank whereby I, as a BMI composer, could get hold of any amount up to the estimated value of my next six quarterly royalties in advance. Eventually, it all came home to roost when I had gotten past all the major expenses of the recovery process, and the monies I was used to collecting were still going straight from BMI to U.S. Bank.

For nearly five years, I found myself locked into a cycle of slowly but surely running through the money I had borrowed before the loan itself was paid off by my royalties, and then having to repeat the pattern; borrow another amount on future royalties, use that to live on, and keep watching as BMI sent my checks directly to the bank. It wasn't a wonderful feeling, but it was definitely worth it. It wasn't anything I had to concern myself with at the time.

My recovery routine started slowly and was purposely made simple and undemanding. There were certain basic things that had to be accomplished before any of the heavy work could begin. Things like being able to stand up—granted, I was doing it with the support of a walker—but at least I was upright.

The first thing on the agenda was to establish my ability to walk with the aid of a walker. The hospital workout area had an indoor walking loop that was about one-hundred and twenty feet in circumference. In my initial routine,

Lame Brain

Helmut had me try to see if I could go a quarter of the way around the track before I had to sit back down in my wheelchair, which always traveled behind me. When I showed I could do that, we upped the ante to a third of a circuit, and then to halfway around the track. Little by little, he worked me up to a complete lap and I started to feel like a real world-beater. I had managed to accomplish all that within three months on a two session per week regimen.

After that, Helmut said we were going to try a little transition work. He took away my walker and gave me a pair of crutches, and made me do the whole shebang all over again. Start with a quarter way around and go a bit further each session until I could navigate the whole track.

Then I was introduced to a much tougher assignment. Helmut asked me to put aside the crutches and go it on my own. Not the whole circuit, of course. A quarter, then a third, then halfway, and eventually all the way around. That took nearly four more months. And of course I always had my wheelchair as my shadow, so I could fall backwards into it if necessary.

At first, it was not a pretty thing to watch. I'm not sure if it looked as awkward as it felt, but I'd be surprised if it didn't. I was staggering more than walking, and the mirrors on the gym wall did nothing to change my mind when I finally dared to look.

As time went by, I began to have more control, and Helmut kept challenging me to do just a little bit more each session. He also started to add exercises that helped me to smooth out my walking gait. It reminded my muscles of what they were supposed to do and how they were meant to work together.

Just to be accurate about my progress, except for my sessions at the gym, I was still wheelchair bound. In a way, it was a love-hate relationship between me and my program. I liked Helmut, but I knew he was never going to let me get comfortable in my exercise routine. Once something on the chart was reasonably easy for me to get through, I could count on the fact that next time something new would be added that would be seemingly beyond my ability. But I knew that was the only way to get where I wanted to go. It was frustrating and liberating at the same time. It was the classic case of "no pain, no gain." Even though there was not much physical pain (aside from when I was on the exercise machines), there was ample mental exertion in trying to direct my body to do what I wanted it to do.

One of the hardest things to do was not to cheat. With most of my exercises, once Helmut had demonstrated how to do it, I was left on my own with no one to monitor me and make sure I did the full count of repetitions or went the full distance. It was a total honor system. Believe me, more than once I was tempted to fudge the numbers or stretch the distance of what I had done for that day. Some of those exercises hurt like hell. Others were exhausting. And every one teetered right on the edge of being more than I was capable of in my abilities.

But I didn't cheat.

At first, it was a matter of ethical behavior. Helmut trusted me to be honest and do what I said I would do. Then it became a point of stubborn pride (or ego) that I could stick it out for the intended duration of each exercise. And before long, it finally sunk in that the whole point of it all was to keep me at the very edge of what I thought was possible. It wasn't supposed to be easy, or comfortable. It was meant to take me just a little further each time.

Theoretically, I'd known that all along. But in practice, when you're straining to do those last five leg lifts, and your thighs feel like they're on fire, you tend to lose the mental aspect of it all.

For the first nine months or so of my therapy, I saw Helmut twice a week. Once I had progressed a little and was actually a tiny bit mobile on my own, I started coming to the hospital gym two or three additional times a week to work on the exercise routine he had worked out for me. Mary would drive me to and from the gym (as it was open for general public membership) and she would do all the one-person exercises right along with me. The others required her to either supervise, or act as my partner. There were several things I had to do in some of the routines that required two participants in different roles.

After that, Helmut moved me forward to some non-demanding but undeniably non-traditional exercises. By that I mean they were not your typical push-ups or jumping jacks type stuff. They were things like having him bounce a softly inflated softball-sized ball to me in various places. He'd go high to the left, high to the right, low to the right, straight at me, etc., but in no particular order or pattern. My job was simply to catch the ball using both hands. The idea was to make my brain respond to changing stimuli with no established sequence. There were also apparently simple things, like standing on my tiptoes or bending as far forward as I could. Helmut would have me walk up a few steps, one at a time. Eventually, we increased my effort to a whole flight of stairs. I was also asked to stand on one foot for as many seconds as I could, and then do the same on the other foot.

One of my favorite exercises was doing a full three-sixty clockwise take two steps, and then do a full three-sixty counter clockwise. I discovered that having somewhat tenuous walking skills to start with can greatly increase the effects of dizziness. I ended up flat on my butt more than once while working on that one.

Before I knew it, eight months had gone by, and even though I was making progress I hadn't improved nearly as much as I had hoped to. About that time, Helmut advanced me to hopping in a small square. Hop forward, then go right, then backward, and finally back to the left. Then I was given the job of skipping across a room.

Most of these exercises might sound incredibly easy and something a three year old could do, but take my word for it—each one was a serious challenge. Another of my favorites that looked quite simple but was actually very hard was catching a large, volleyball-sized ball after bouncing it off a wall. I know

Lame Brain

I struggled with nearly every new addition to my regimen, but eventually I managed to master them to my own and Helmut's satisfaction. There were so many different exercises I'm not able to remember more than a few that have stuck in my mind.

There was almost always a learning process nestled behind the activities. At one point Helmut added the discipline of having me walk up a fairly gentle incline, but for the first few times we did it, he'd send me back down in my wheelchair. Initially, I thought that was because he didn't want to tire me out. One day when I said I'd walk back down, he said I wasn't quite ready for that yet. When I asked why, he told me that walking uphill or downhill used two entirely different sets of muscles, and we hadn't started on my downhill set yet.

And just because I managed to succeed at an exercise for a few sessions didn't mean I had added that particular skill to my repertoire. That may have been the most frustrating aspect of the whole deal. I learned that difficult lesson early on in my attempt at recovery. Very few other injuries require the same treatment as a brain injury, or the same attitude.

When you break your arm, they set the bone, put a cast on it, and as time passes, slowly but steadily, it heals. They take off the cast, and you go on with your life. Simple. Brain injuries don't work that way. There's nothing steady about it. When you attempt to fix a broken brain, you can never count on any progress you make to be a "mission accomplished."

One day I repeatedly found myself starting my routine and being unable to do something that I had mastered (I thought) weeks earlier. I had to go back and master the skill all over again. That made it very hard to sustain any hope that I could ever recover.

* * *

It took between six months and a year after I started therapy to progress from the wheelchair to a walker in my civilian life on a full time basis. I still kept the chair around, because I got tired pretty easily. Helmut had told me early on that a person begins to lose significant musculature after two weeks of being off their feet, and since I had gone well over a year before I even started my program, my musculature was pretty much shot to hell. My routine was extremely varied with everything from the walking to the ball exercises to a dozen other activities in between. Walking up and down stairs, stepping onto a foot-high platform, up and down twenty times, alternating leg lifts, head turns while walking, standing entirely on my toes alone and then on my heels, squats, sudden weight shifts, forward and backwards, walking with crossover steps, and the list goes on…

Later on, we got into more seemingly simple things that most people would never dream of as being difficult, but take it from me, they are *extremely* hard to do when you're learning how to walk again. I'm talking about such little gems as one-footed jumping, lurches (I won't try to explain what those are. If you know, you know. If not, you need to see them, not read them), and the aforementioned ball toss, only this time with the additional element of standing on a squishy foam pad. Hell, even catching a ball without any fancy stuff had been a skill I was challenged to relearn after my injury. And then there were the machines...

* * *

Helmut told me that recovering my agility was only half the project. Considering how long I'd been off my feet, my legs were close to useless when I started, and only a little more serviceable several months in. As soon as I had showed I could walk even a little, I was started on an exercise machine regimen to augment the exercises. These were meant to increase the strength I had lost, both in my legs and my upper body. It turns out that whatever strength I had added in the arms and shoulders by my initial practice of levering myself onto the couch and bed had largely faded once I was in a wheelchair. I know many people seem to increase their upper body strength when they are put in a wheelchair, but I never propelled myself that vigorously.

I had to do leg curls, leg presses, leg lifts, and once I was able to walk a bit better, I was put on the elliptical and the treadmill (backwards and forwards). There were even machines specifically designed for my thighs. With them, I had to press the pads together a bunch of times, then reverse the process and pull the pads apart a bunch more times.

I have to admit, I never did manage to make the Stairmaster work for me. There were even toe presses (straighten your legs on the leg press and then lift your artificially increased weight with your toes). And for my upper body, there were the wall pulleys and the rowing machine.

On all the machines, as soon as I was comfortable with a given weight it was increased. Once I could do the required number of repetitions, I was asked to do ten more. By now, my solo sessions were keeping me in the hospital gym for about two-and-a-half hours a trip. With Helmut, they were usually a little shorter because he spent an hour with me and wore me out enough that another hour was about all I could do on my own.

* * *

I found out midway through my therapy that my legs had forgotten how to run. It was infuriating and frightening to finally be able to walk without too much trouble and then to have my brain give the command to my legs to pick up the pace to have nothing happen. The signal was not getting through.

It's difficult to put into words, but my legs just wouldn't respond when I tried

Lame Brain

to make them do my bidding. They call the process brain command, muscle response. And mine didn't work. But the brain command is somewhere below the conscious level. Stop and think about it. Just exactly how do you *tell* yourself to run? I never had to work it out before. I just did it. When I discovered my inability, it was the most helpless I had felt since the first day I climbed out of bed, collapsed, and couldn't get up.

Even though running was not really part of the program, I took it upon myself to make that one of my long-term goals. The only way I could figure out how to approach it was to start by just walking faster. Then I tried to lift my legs a little more, and stretch out my stride. I expanded things by starting to push off of my front foot each time I brought my back foot forward. I may not be explaining this very well, but that was exactly my problem. I was having trouble explaining it to myself.

It took me another month or two, but eventually I was able to jog down the forty-foot hall. I added that to my routine, and did eight lengths of the hall every session. I chose the hall as opposed to going outside because the hall was carpeted and my balance was still an ongoing adventure when I was pushing the pace. I could easily have done a face plant on a concrete sidewalk. So let's just say that wasn't on my dance card, and I didn't have any desire to add it.

As I got further into things Helmut found a new way to challenge me. Multi-tasking. The first thing I was asked to do was walk around the track while bouncing a ball to myself. Once I got that down, it was time to change hands every other bounce. That was still not too much of a stretch because I could look at the ground while I was performing the act. But it got trickier when Helmut asked me to throw the ball up in the air and catch it as I walked the track. I could no longer keep track of my feet while I moved forward.

As I write about this now, all of these exercises seem ridiculously easy to me. But that's from my present point of view. It only takes a minute to cast my mind back to how I saw things back then. At the time I was trying to master them, the tasks seemed nearly impossible.

* * *

Back on the home front (where I spent the rest of my time), it took a while longer than I had promised Mary I'd get around to it, but we finally engaged a home caregiver service three days a week so she could continue to work. By this point, it was really important that she stay employed, because almost all my money (the loans against royalties) was being used up in the pursuit of my recovery and our basic living expenses. Without part of the medical expenses being covered by the insurance her job provided, it would have been too much to manage.

Initially, we went through a couple of caregivers very quickly. John was the first guy, but he stopped working as a caregiver about a month after I signed up, so then Steve took his place.

Steve's main line of work was teaching history, and he brought that teacher's mentality to my situation. At my house, between hospital visits, he kept trying to add to the exercise regimen Helmut had set up for me, as well as offering endless suggestions while Helmut and I were in the middle of a session. The two of them didn't even know one another except through me, so of course they weren't working together. That was very confusing, because Steve was a caregiver, not a physical therapist. I imagine the unsolicited assistance was annoying to Helmut, as I know it was to me.

He had that teacher's ingrained habit of always asking his client (or student) to make themselves do a little more than they were capable of doing. That probably serves a good purpose in the classroom, but it isn't quite as workable an idea when you're dealing with physical therapy issues. My overview of the way to approach my recovery was to always challenge myself, but never *push* myself. When you push yourself, you increase the risk of further injury.

I know he didn't do it intentionally, but I always felt I was under the gun with him. It was not so much that he pushed me physically. It was more of a mental thing. He was always talking to me about how by now I should be out of my chair and walking up and down the stairs without any help, and other little things like that. I couldn't help but feel I was not giving it all I could, even though I knew I was.

He was an extremely intelligent man and a really nice guy, so I was reluctant to ask for a different caregiver. He was also willing to go the extra yard and come when we called him for help on a couple of occasions, even though he wasn't on the clock.

It all worked out in the end, because he was offered a teaching position, and had to resign from the agency. At that point, I was sent Valerie Elmy, who was just what I needed. She had a marvelous personality, and always encouraged me to try my best at whatever I was doing. At the same time, she was very relaxed about it, and I never felt pressured.

There were also a couple of side benefits, because Val loved to cook and clean, which made things easier for Mary, too. And as a bonus, Val loved my music. Little things like that were an added motivation to fight my way back, knowing there were people that appreciated what I had to offer. She also gave me one of the best pieces of advice I ever got about recovery. She told me that one of the main dangers for people who are injured and can get better is that after they have been incapacitated for a while they can get used to depending on others for everything, and end up preferring to be waited on all the time over doing things for themselves.

She told me she didn't think I had that kind of personality, but that I should keep my guard up about it in case I started getting too comfortable. It was solid advice. All I had to do was remember back before I started therapy and I could see how the combination of knowing the difficulty of changing anything, plus how deceptively attractive it is to be waited on hand and foot, and I could see how for some people that might be a very appealing option. But only in the short term. For me, having everything essential at my beck and call would soon pale compared to what wasn't available.

So I guess she was right about me not having that kind of personality. Maybe my inability to accept my situation gracefully would be a flaw out there in the so-called normal (?) world, hinting as it did of a controlling personality, but in my battle to regain the use of my legs, it was one of the best qualities I could have asked for.

That Other Thing

Chapter Five

Many years before either my brain injury or my marriage to Mary, I began my first safari into Lame Land and I did it without anyone pressuring me to make the trip. Of course, I didn't know where I was headed when I started, and in fact, my tour guide on the expedition was only a secondary background force at the beginning of the journey. That was the sneaky part of the equation.

While I was keeping up my guard against getting too fond of all the high profile evils, I got sucker punched by something I wasn't paying enough attention to. Despite all the fooling around and experimentation I indulged myself in with all the ogres of the drug world, the drug that I had the longest struggle with was good old, totally legal, demon rum. And vodka. And tequila. And just about anything else in a bottle except for beer—for which I never developed a taste. And I should have known better, because I'd seen what could happen right in my own family. But I'm getting ahead of myself...

There was one drug I didn't keep in check. Cocaine. But at least that one was a kind of trade-off, and offered something in return.

I first used cocaine shortly after I got involved in the main arena of rock and roll music, and by the time I got to the most successful days of my career, I was using quite a large amount of the drug. That probably doesn't come as any big surprise. Rock in the '70s pretty much lived up to its reputation, and I was certainly not flying solo as a cocaine fiend.

But I still believe that my motivation was a little different than most other people I knew that did cocaine. When my friends would get high, the only thing they wanted to do was go out and party. What I wanted was to go off by myself with a guitar. My rationale was that I did most of my composing when I was high, and I managed to write a lot of songs while under the influence, several of which hit the charts. Maybe I would have written some of those songs anyway, but there's no way to know for sure. I have often told friends that I am one of a very small segment of the drug-using society who can say I turned a profit on cocaine without ever dealing it. In spite of the enormous amount of money I spent on coke, my songs have provided me with an equal or larger return over the years, thanks to my publishing royalties.

In conjunction with the coke, I began to drink. Not a whole lot, but more than I had prior to that, which was not at all. The alcohol served as a downer—something to help ease me back down after I had been cruising along on a coke high for a couple of days—when I needed a break for a little while.

Just a word about that. On the occasions when I actually found really pure cocaine, it wasn't the sleep depriving, jacked up, teeth grinding, speedy trip that most people associate with the drug. It was actually a blissful, spacier kind of high. Don't take that to mean I'm in favor of the drug or promoting its use; I'm simply trying to clarify a widely held misconception.

Anyway, what was usually available on the street had been cut with various things that made it a whole different animal. When I finished a binge and was coming off the drug, I could usually count on lying awake for hours, if not all night. My mind would still be going at a frantic rate but thinking in such a fragmented jumble that the process of coming down was a form of extended torture. Booze could usually cut through the buzz and help me get some rest. I tried valiums and Quaaludes, but nothing else did the trick like alcohol did, and anyway, pills were something I was not inclined to get too heavily tangled up with.

There was a good reason for that. My mother got heavily into pills when I was a kid. She chose sleeping pills, the red Placidils to be exact, and ended up trading those little darlings for a serious alcohol addiction. I'm pleased to say she managed to shake her problem. When she passed away in 1998, she had seventeen years and counting of sobriety.

The thing was, my mom had gotten involved with alcohol by what might be called an accident, too. Or bad advice. She began taking pills due to the amount of stress she was under. She was trying to juggle the demands of being a mother while also working full time and sharing many of the responsibilities of running the family business. As a result, she was having a lot of difficulty sleeping, and started taking the pills to get a little rest. But as time went by, she began to develop quite a tolerance for the drug and soon she found herself eating the pills like candy. Eventually, she went to a doctor for help and he strongly suggested she get off the pills. He said that the next time she felt like popping another Placidil, she should have a beer instead.

My father told me years later that the doctor was very lucky that he didn't do the man bodily harm when he heard about the recommendation.

A few months after consulting the doctor, my mom was still taking the pills, but now she had developed a liquor habit (mostly beer) to go with it. My father tried to tell her she was on the verge of becoming an alcoholic hand-in-hand with her pill addiction, but she laughed it off.

With a smile on her face, she asked, "How can you think I'm an alcoholic when I never even touch the hard stuff? I just have a few beers to calm down when I'm feeling a little tense."

So my dad reluctantly backed away from suggesting she was turning into an alky. At one point though, I overheard him ask a friend if there was such a thing as a beer-oholic.

It went on for a couple of years like that with Mom able to hide it from almost everyone else but the family. Then, finally the day came when she realized things were getting so far out of her control that she was risking the loss of her marriage and her family.

She decided she wanted to do something serious about changing her behavior, so she voluntarily committed herself to the Florida State Hospital, a mental institution in Arcadia, Florida. They hadn't come up with the concept of rehab centers yet so institutionalizing oneself was the only available choice.

We went to visit her every weekend during her three-month stay. The hospital was a perfect example of not judging a book by its cover. Outside, the campus was a lovely sprawling expanse of green lawns and stately university style buildings, but once you got inside you were confronted with the bars on the windows and the institutional green paint on the walls. There was no overlooking the fact either that you were in a detention facility. Without doubt, that experience was a major chapter in my extra-curricular education.

Within about four or five weeks my mother had become a trustee at the hospital, responsible for looking after other more dramatically impaired patients. As a result, I was exposed to the first *truly* abnormal behavior I had ever seen up close. I won't go into the things I saw. It was too devastating, and I'm not intending to turn those tragic situations into a source of humor. But the things I observed there will stay with me forever.

Most of the patients there were really seriously disturbed, and some of the things they did were pretty comical. I admit I laughed at things I saw more than once. I was grateful my mom was dealing with her problem and that it wasn't even in the same league as some of those folks. Though, underneath it all I felt very sorry for them. I just wanted my mother to get better, and luckily she had the same plan.

When Mom finally came home, she had freed herself from her dependence on pills. However, it was a long time before she was able to shake the doctor's suggestion to 'have a beer'. And, as you have probably heard, there is a tendency towards a genetic predisposition to alcoholism. Or as they say 'it runs in the family.' And true or not, I know you couldn't use me as an example to disprove the statement.

You might ask why I was unwilling to get involved with pills, but jumped right into alcohol. Good question. I think it was because of all my childhood experiences watching my mom use pills. The fact that long after the stress factor had been dealt with, she was still taking them. As far as I could tell, her

Lame Brain

main purpose at that point was to get wasted, and that's how I perceived pills in general. When I started to drink, it was only to mitigate the effects of something else. Just like my mother.

And besides, with my mom, even though she hurt herself just as much—if not more—with booze, I still saw the pills as the original villain in her situation. Even so, I did have some reservations (which I definitely managed to overcome) about liquor.

I never even had my first sip of alcohol until I was eighteen. It was at a college fraternity party and there were extenuating circumstances, including the blind date the fraternity insisted on setting me up with that night. Suffice it to say, the young lady and I were not a very good match. So I got incredibly drunk and sick on the unlikely combination of scotch and Sprite. That experience was enough to keep me from taking my next drink for another three years.

For a long time, I was only an occasional drinker apart from the time when I was consuming coke, and in those situations, I only drank enough to take the edge off. Even when I did imbibe socially, it was rarely to excess. But as time went by, the boundaries kept getting hazier.

Years later (early '90s), there came a point when I found the songs had stopped coming so easily when I did my blow, and that when I simply gave it up. Surprisingly, I didn't have that much of a struggle letting the cocaine go.

The liquor was another story.

And before I go any further in my own journey, I want to tell you that the things I'm about to be relating are not meant to be 'This is why I drank' stories, like the ones often heard from the guy on the next bar stool. I was drinking for no reason except that I had gotten into the habit, and I liked the buzz. And that's no reason at all.

* * *

My alcohol intake was slowly but steadily increasing while I was still using cocaine, and by the time I left Firefall, it was getting to be a very noticeable problem. Noticeable to everyone but me, that is.

I gave my notice to the band in August of 1981. We were finishing a tour with a couple of shows in Hawaii, the last of which was on Maui where we played at the tennis stadium outside of Lahaina. It was clear to me by that point that the special something the band once had was all but gone. I think maybe things were starting to lose momentum after the *Élan* album, but they had really changed drastically when Mark Andes and Michael Clarke left after *Undertow*, even though Michael's leaving had not been entirely his choice. He had his own alcohol thing going. And the last album we had done, *Clouds Across the Sun*, we could have mailed in.

After resigning from the band in Hawaii, I went home to Boulder where I had to deal with yet another unexpected change. I'd been renting my house on 16th Street for about four years, and I really loved the place.

I suppose I could include a bunch of the stories about things that happened while I lived there, but I think I'll just say it was a good place for me to be during that time in my life, and a wonderful place to come home to after long bouts on the road. In a quiet, residential area, it was close to town and only a few blocks from Colorado University. A lot of well-educated people lived in the area, including numerous professors and grad students, so there was a kind of loose, live and let live attitude to the neighborhood. Very liberal and liberated. It also made for better conversation in the checkout line at the market.

Jack, the owner, had put my residence up for sale almost a year before, but there hadn't been any serious offers as far as I knew. Jack had promised me that since I had been such a good tenant, when and if the house sold, one way or the other I would have a minimum of three months to vacate.

As it turned out, he sold the house to a college student while I was away on my last tour in Hawaii. Some dad had bought it for junior, and the kid wanted to take possession by the time school started, or in about two weeks' time.

So here was my situation. I had bought a house in California about a year earlier, but had not gotten around to spending any time there. I had just quit my band and needed to vacate my residence *pronto*. I was considering trying to have a solo career again, and one of the centers of the music industry was Los Angeles. It seemed pretty clear that all the signs were suggesting I pull up stakes, leave Colorado behind, and make the move back to the West Coast.

So that's what I did. I left the Rocky Mountains and the life I had had there behind me, including all the people I cared about, and moved to my house in Malibu Lake.

Shortly after I arrived, I got slammed by a number of unexpected fresh problems in my new life, starting with being advised by my lawyers to lay low for a while musically. It seems there were some legal vulnerabilities left over from the band, and I was the prime potential target. I was also made aware of a huge IRS indemnity due to some very questionable shenanigans by one of my business advisors. That, in and of itself, probably would have been enough to start me drinking if I hadn't already had a well-established habit.

The tax thing came out of nowhere. My phone rang one morning about 7 A.M. and the conversation went something like this.

"Hello?"
"Mr. Roberts?"
"Yes?"
"Mr. Rick Roberts?"
"Yes!"
"Mr. Richard J. Roberts?"
"Yes, who's this?"

"Mr. Richard J. Roberts, the singer?"

"*YES! WHO IS THIS!?*"

Then came the crusher. "This is Agent Smith (I can't remember his actual name) of the IRS."

My first thought was *Oh my God. They've caught me.*

My second thought was *Wait a minute. For what?*

He answered my unasked question. "Are you aware that you owe approximately $241,000 for the years 1977, 1978, and 1979?"

(Small choking noises came from my end of the phone.) "No, (cough) no I wasn't aware of that. How could I possibly owe that much? I don't think I even *made* that much during those years!"

"Yes, well we received no returns from you for those three years. And there have been significant penalties and interest, bringing the total to that amount."

I was decimated. Having a bombshell like this dropped in my lap was something I would never have imagined in my worst nightmares. And it happened so suddenly, I couldn't even process the effect it was going to have on my life for a long time to come. Twenty years, as it turned out. All I could think of right then was that when I combined this information and what my lawyers had told me about keeping a low profile and not starting any new musical projects, I was truly between a rock and a hard place.

That's what I meant about *shenanigans*. I was on the road touring for a significant part of those years, and the people who handled my business affairs did my taxes. They did the bookwork and all I did was come in and sign my name. Then they would file the documents. Or, at least that's how I thought the procedure was supposed to work. Somehow the returns never arrived at the IRS office. Maybe I was the one who was supposed to do the actual mailing, but that's not the way I remember it. I suppose I should have been monitoring my finances more closely, but I was more interested in my musical endeavors than my bank balances.

It was not a good situation to find myself in. I had no close friends to lean on. They were all back in Boulder. Subsequently, I kept doing cocaine and began to drink even more. I wound up spending ten years in California residing at seven different addresses before circumstances brought me back to Boulder again.

Love Is Strange

Sad to say, I wasn't involved with anyone on a romantic level and wasn't close enough to my family right then so I had no one to help me keep things in perspective. During that whole ten years in California, I was involved with only one serious relationship, which began with a world of wonderful possibilities, but turned out to be a disaster before it was over.

It happened at the end of 1983 when I decided to take a trip back to Boulder. Henry and Susie Hester, two good, long-time friends, invited me to be their houseguest while I was in town. I had only been back for a day or two when I met a woman.

Her name was Loretta, and she was amazing. She was a willowy strawberry blond, with huge blue eyes. It was obvious from the outset she was very intelligent, had a great sense of humor, and a deep, husky voice that was almost too sexy to be legal. I was immediately smitten.

She was seemingly quite taken by me, too, and from the moment I met her, we started to move in the direction of love. I say 'move in the direction of' because, despite what I might have said in some of my songs, I'm pretty skeptical about the idea of love at first sight. I'm a total believer in *lust* at first sight though, and I was definitely in that.

Later that same afternoon, she took me over to the house of a friend of hers who was out of town. We soaked in his hot tub for a while, and then later, availed ourselves of her friend's bed. When I got back to Henry and Susie's, I told them all about my new acquaintance. They were less than ecstatic.

Henry took me aside and flat out said, "Stay away from that woman! She's *crazy!*"

I told him she didn't seem at all crazy to me, and asked him why he would think that. He told me that she had burned her last boyfriend's house down after they had split up. I asked him how he knew, and he only said to trust him, he knew.

I persisted in saying I didn't see how that could be true, because if it was, why hadn't she been prosecuted? There had been no witnesses, he said.

"Then how can you be so sure?" I asked.

He continued to answer simply by saying, "I just know, that's all."

We had quite a big argument about it, and he told me she was not welcome in his house. I got on my high horse and told him I was going to relocate back to town. Upon hearing I was no longer staying with my friends, Loretta invited me to stay with her. I immediately accepted.

The next few days were spent in a haze of alcohol and sex with a fair smattering of cocaine, just to keep things lively. I soon discovered she was one of the most accomplished lovers I had ever been with in bed. During that span, I spent almost all my time with my new paramour, but curiously enough when I was out and about alone, several old friends told me the same story about her pyro-maniacal proclivities. Being a young man on the verge of falling in love, I figured the best thing to do was to ask Loretta outright.

I went straight to her and told her what people were saying. She looked a little hurt to know that she was thought of that way and said, "Isn't that weird? I've heard that same thing. I can't imagine where they ever got that idea."

Lame Brain

And since I *was* that same young man, teetering on the brink of love, the issue was settled as far I was concerned. It never occurred to me that she hadn't actually answered my question.

Spoiler alert: A few years later, one of my Boulder friends told me he had actually seen her running from the scene of the crime, but due to some legal vulnerability of his own, he couldn't come forward. He's the one who had told my friend, Henry, and had sworn him to secrecy.

I decided to stay a few weeks longer in Colorado, meanwhile falling completely in love. By the time I was ready to go, I had invited Loretta to move in with me in Malibu Lake. We arranged it so she would tie up her loose ends in Boulder and then join me about a month later.

Maybe I would have paid more attention if I'd been a little less toasted, a little less often, but I ignored several warning signs, as well as the advice of my friends. I didn't know it yet, but 1984 would be full of surprises, and Loretta would be a big part of most all of them.

The Gathering Storm

Chapter Six

I arrived back in California shortly after New Year's of 1984 with some very mixed emotions going through my head. On the one hand, I was filled with all the giddiness and high spirits that almost always seem to come with falling in love. On the other hand, I couldn't hide from the fact that my ongoing tax liabilities and my monthly overhead—what with my big, mostly empty house—were doing eating away at my financial stability.

I had managed to arrange a payment plan with the IRS to satisfy my indemnity to them, but it was rather an expensive set up. I was required to pay them $500 a month and $5000 every quarter with the arrival of each royalty check. If you do the math for that arrangement, it comes out to $26,000 a year. That meant I would be able to get clear of my IRS obligation in less than ten years (that's just a little joke). Except that once you're on a payment plan, the penalties may stop, but the interest is a gift that keeps on giving. It would have been a debt that lasted a lifetime, if not for one good man. I'll explain that later.

The only significant income I had was my quarterly royalty checks, even though I had started performing again. What little profit I generated by playing was hardly enough to mention. I wasn't doing many gigs, and overall, my overhead was far exceeding my income. I was sending some financial support to my mother throughout this time, but that wasn't enough to make a difference, and even if it had been, I don't think I could have brought myself to cut her off. Believe it or not, another major contributor to my overhead was VHS rentals. On top of every other unsettling aspect of my return to California, there was no cable available in Malibu Lake and the local TV reception was awful. So I got into the habit of going down to the video store and renting at least three movies every day. At about $4 a film, I was amazed at how quickly the costs turned into a major expenditure.

Meanwhile, I was still spending a lot of money on cocaine, and continuing to drink too much. Actually it was more than that. In hindsight, I can see that my financial troubles, my frustration with my musical situation, and the feeling

Lame Brain

of isolation in my new surroundings had begun to take a toll beyond what I realized then. Combining all those elements with the uncertainty of a new love relationship had me very scared as well as incredibly stressed. I wasn't just drinking too much. Drinking had become an essential part of my day to day existence.

Financially, I found I had fallen into a vicious cycle that didn't look like it was going to change any time soon. Each time a check arrived, I would immediately pay out the larger part of it just to cover existing obligations (including the omnipresent IRS liability), and by the month before the next one was due, I'd be scraping bottom trying to make ends meet until that one came, and the whole cycle started again. I didn't really realize just how serious the situation was, but when I returned home from Colorado, I found out rather abruptly.

When I arrived back in L.A. from my Boulder trip and my new-found romance, I grabbed a cab out to Malibu Lake. I was totally tapped out on cash, so I told the driver we needed to take a detour by my bank. I had to get some money to pay his fare, as well as to have some cash in hand so I could get some groceries and stock up the refrigerator.

Malibu Lake was located away from anything in the way of businesses, and I was banking several miles away in Calabasas. When we got to the bank, I had the taxi wait while I went inside to make a withdrawal. I wrote out a check, and gave it to the teller, who started to process it. But then she stopped and informed me that my funds had been garnished and my account was closed.

I have no recollection of who had claimed my money, which I can only attribute to a combination of shock, and in a broader sense, selective memory loss. Or maybe just spending too much time in the ozone. It wasn't a monumental amount of money, around $2,000 as I recall, but it was a very big blow at the moment, especially because my taxi fare was already nearly seventy bucks!

I expected I was in for a pretty nasty situation when I told the facts to the driver. (I once drove a cab for a little while, and it had been my experience that very few drivers will respond too well to being stiffed on that big a fare.)

I went back out to the taxi and explained my situation to the driver. He was incredibly kind. He could see by how pale I was that I was telling him the truth, and not trying to hustle him. I said I didn't have any money to pay him. He graciously told me he would take me home, gave me his card, and I could pay him later when I got everything straightened out.

Luckily, I was due to get a new royalty check within the next week or so, and when I did, of course the first thing I took out was his fare, plus what was hopefully one of the biggest tips he would get for quite a while, and put it in the mail.

Of course, I chose to open my new bank account with a different bank, in Malibu this time. It was a little farther to go, but there was no way I was going back to those guys in Calabasas. They hadn't done anything wrong, but I knew

I would never have felt comfortable going there again. Call it a quirk.

The month between my rather unsettling return home and Loretta's arrival dragged by slowly. It gave me some time to reassess the situation I was getting myself into. If I could barely get along as a one man show, would it really be possible to support myself and a woman?

When I sat down and divvied up my latest royalty check, I got even more nervous about the future. Once I had planned out my three-month overhead, including my normal monthly bills, the mortgage, the IRS, and a responsible amount for day-to-day living expenses, I found I was looking at a very hard last few weeks before another check time came around again.

I called Loretta and told her that since it was going to be slim pickings for a while, she might want to either wait to come, or reconsider entirely. She assured me that the finances didn't matter, and we would make it work somehow. She assured me that I wouldn't have to shoulder the entire financial burden by myself, because she was going to start looking for a job as soon as she arrived—she had a lot of skills to bring to the table that she hadn't even shown me yet.

I let myself be convinced without putting up much of a fight, because she was telling me what I wanted to hear. I have to say though, things were not going the way I had planned as far as how I would welcome my new love. Little did I know I would actually be welcoming two people into my life, and one of them was named Ms. Hyde.

Meet Ms. Hyde

Loretta flew into Burbank Airport where I picked her up on a chilly evening late in February. I remember feeling a little off balance trying to start a new chapter in my life at an airport that didn't seem part of Los Angeles. In spite of all the traveling I had done in my L.A. years with the Burrito Brothers and since I'd come back to Southern Cal, I don't think I had ever been to any of the airports in the area except Los Angeles International (LAX). I'd seen the planes flying in or out from Burbank every time I drove down Highway 101, but I'd never had any reason to actually go there.

It gave the whole scene a slightly surreal feeling. I guess I was also uneasy about starting out with so much financial uncertainty about the immediate future. In hindsight, maybe it was a premonition.

After we set up housekeeping, Loretta started looking for work. Meanwhile, I went on harassing my agent about booking me some more shows, whether around the area, or anywhere else it was offered. He did manage to find me a few gigs, but nothing to write home about. I managed to cut back on my cocaine intake and that helped to remove one drain on our resources. But the alcohol continued to flow for both of us.

Meanwhile, Loretta got a job in one of the classier department stores in Thousand Oaks. They hired her in the woman's fashion section, and she quickly rose through the ranks. She was soon the assistant manager of her department. I wasn't surprised. As she had promised, she had a lot of various skills, and she was quite stylish.

Even so, our money situation continued to be a concern. After a few months, the tension began to mount. Every now and then, and seemingly with no instigation beyond some off-hand remark, Loretta would fly into a tremendous rage and start screaming at me, and throwing things in my direction.

I attributed it to the monetary pressures we were under, but it was a little scary seeing her react that way. After a while, she would calm down and go on as if nothing had happened. Without doubt, the drinking and drugging didn't help, but her outbursts didn't correlate directly to that. It was just as likely to happen when we'd been staying straight and sober as it did when we were high.

And somewhat more disturbing was the fact that she had shown me one episode of the same behavior back in Boulder.

At the time, I thought it was just an aberration, or the result of alcohol, but it upset me so much I grabbed my shoulder bag and my guitar and started out the door. Loretta caught me in the parking lot, and literally got down on her knees to apologize and beg me to come back. That was one of the warning signs I shouldn't have ignored.

As time went by, it got worse. I had a fairly large collection of artwork at the time, including a whole portfolio of original Edward Curtis prints, and during several of her tantrums, she ripped up some of the pieces. She knew which ones were my favorites, and those were the ones she targeted.

I had already framed some of them, and I don't think any of those survived. She smashed the glass and ripped up the picture without skipping a beat.

But even among the unframed portraits, she picked out the ones I held the dearest. I have to admit, I found it very curious that in a situation where she was otherwise totally out of control, she still had enough presence of mind to remember to which of my collection I was most attached. I would have expected her to go for whatever was within easy reach, but she sometimes went to an entirely different part of the house to get to her target. It was very scary. What was most confusing about Loretta was that she was wonderful most of the time. I didn't have a clue about what was likely to set her off. It was almost like I had fallen in love with Dr. Jekyll, and from time to time, Ms. Hyde would show up.

I couldn't help but think of the old nursery rhyme about *"there was a little girl, who had a little curl, right in the middle of her forehead. When she was good, she was very, very good, but when she was bad, she was horrid!"**

---

*Magic Mother Goose Melodies (1879).

Rick Roberts

* * *

I started drinking even more during those months, and for the only time I can remember, before or since, I was drinking with the definite intention of getting plastered. I was in a relationship I no longer wanted to be in, but I couldn't bring myself to pull the trigger to kick her out, either. My resolve had been diluted by the combination of alcohol and the guilt of bringing her out to a place where she had no one but me.

Long Day's Journey Into Night

Chapter Seven

In time, Loretta developed a habit of hiding one or another of my guitars. When I would ask if she knew where it was, she claimed she knew nothing about it. Since we were both drinking quite a bit and still doing a small amount of cocaine, she told me I was probably just imagining things and had put the instrument down somewhere else and spaced out having done so. Even though I was certain that was not what was happening, I didn't feel I could make that convincing a case for any other possibility in light of the fact that I *was* getting pretty high, pretty often. In retrospect, I think that even when we were straight, our whole relationship was doomed from the start by the ongoing altered states where we were spending so much of our time. The frequent discussions about the whereabouts of my guitars was good evidence of that.

It was getting pretty obvious to me that unless we got some help or some counseling, our situation would be past saving before long. The thing that made it so difficult to end the relationship was, as I said, for extended periods, she was delightful. Then, at some unimportant or imagined provocation, she'd freak out again. I kept on hoping that as things got better financially, she might stop having these rages. Combining love and liquor can definitely distort your objectivity.

Then one evening when she was due back from work I got a call from the co-worker who usually brought her home. She told me that Loretta had been detained by store security for attempting to walk out with an expensive dress at the end of her workday without paying for it. There was a security chip on the dress, so she had to have known they'd catch her.

I called the store, and a security staff woman confirmed the story. When I asked where Loretta was, I was told they had simply decided to fire her on the spot and cut her loose. The woman said Loretta had told them she was going to hitch hike home.

It took a minute for me to register that part, because at first I was simply relieved she hadn't been arrested for shoplifting. Then the hitchhiking part hit home.

Thousand Oaks, and the mall where the store was located, were about twenty miles from my house. Half the distance was along the 101 freeway, and the rest was a trip up Kanan Road into the mountainous area around the lake. It was most assuredly not a good route for anyone, particularly a solitary woman, to try and catch a ride, especially at night.

I immediately got in my car and started tracing her route home in reverse. Once I got out to Highway 101, I pulled off at the exits to see if I could spot her along the roadside. It was illegal to thumb on the freeway itself, even if you could get someone to stop. Besides, that section of highway wasn't lit, and it was well after dark. At least at the interchanges she'd be visible.

I tried every exit with no success, and eventually gave up and went back home. When I arrived, she was there and immediately asked me where *I* had been.

Before I could answer, she told me that she had quit her job because they were all a bunch of assholes. I couldn't believe she would think she could bluff her way through it, but at least her apparent nonchalance about the event made it easy to see that it was past the point of knowing we 'needed help with the situation.' Not only did something have to be done, but it couldn't be put off any longer.

I told her that I already knew what had happened at the store, and had been out looking for her. I said I thought she should talk to someone and get some counseling. I told her I loved her, but this was way beyond my level of psychological expertise, and definitely out of control.

Her response was to get furious and start yelling.

"Are you saying I'm crazy?" she asked. "I'm not crazy, or at least I'm not as crazy as you are."

She refused to even consider the idea at first, but eventually she calmed down. At that point she was still very reluctant, but she told me she would try a few therapy sessions on the condition that I agreed to see someone, too.

The thing was, I really did love her, and it was important to me to do everything I could to help her get straightened out. With that in mind, I consented.

The next day I made some phone calls, found two willing psychoanalysts, and set up sessions for both of us. As fate would have it, they both worked in the same building. I realized it probably wouldn't be a bad thing for me to talk to someone anyway. I was willing to admit, if only to myself, that no problem in a relationship is the fault of one person alone. Considering how much I was drinking, this might be a blessing in disguise. It was certainly something I couldn't afford to ignore, and it might just benefit us both.

We both did the sessions for about three months, at which time my doctor, who knew I was partially there so that Loretta would come, told me he didn't see any reason for me to continue my sessions with him just to humor her. He told me that my alcohol problem would be better served by someone who was more conversant in that area.

Meanwhile, Loretta told me at almost the same time that she'd decided she didn't want to go to any more therapy sessions. She said the shrink wasn't helping her and didn't understand who she really was. I found out later that her analyst had told Loretta she didn't *want* to see *her* anymore because she wasn't cooperating with the therapy plan and was very hostile.

Actually, I had to admit there *had* been something of a change in things. I had cut way down on my drug and alcohol intake, and Loretta had been calmer than usual. I can only speculate, but I thought maybe Loretta was benefitting by way of getting out some anger and aggression in her sessions. She'd also found another job at a restaurant in Malibu.

I started thinking that we had turned the corner. Things were looking up on the job front for me, too. I was getting a few more bookings, and was able to use my time more constructively. As I said, I had started to think maybe we were going to be able to make a go of things after all.

They say that hope springs eternal. As time passed, it turned out we had just taken a breather, and in the long run, nothing really changed. Loretta's rages returned in top form, and so did my drinking. She lost her job at the restaurant, and it was harder than ever to predict her mood swings.

I went out on a couple of short musical runs, and while I was traveling, I was able to take my mind completely off my domestic problems. But that might not have been such a good thing. It lulled me into a false sense of wellbeing. Then, when I got home, I would find that things were primed to pick up right where they had left off. And, of course, my way to respond to the situation was to pick up the bottle.

While all this turmoil was occupying most of my attention, I was still trying to get something more permanent going musically. For the most part it was pretty frustrating, because somewhere in my subconscious I was still aware of the specter of potential lawsuits and couldn't give it my best shot. And the troubles that were dominating my domestic scene made it even harder to concentrate on my music.

* * *

In my mind, I made a little checklist. I had cut way down on my cocaine. The psychiatrist thing hadn't panned out. I had even tried calling Loretta's family in Ohio at one point, asking them if they might be willing to have her come and stay with them for a while so she could get a little break from the pressures in her life. When they emphatically refused the opportunity, I found I was running out of options and answers. And the stress level at home was getting more and more unbearable every day. At least it was for me. I was constantly walking on eggshells. To say the least, I was in something of a quandary.

I never knew when I might say the wrong thing, push her buttons, and start the fireworks again. It was getting clearer and clearer that I needed to end the relationship as soon as possible, if only for the sake of my own health. I waited for what seemed like a good moment and told her we needed to talk.

So, we sat down and I tried to get her to agree with me that we had obviously made a mistake. It was plain things were not working out between us.

But that was a wasted effort. She knew all the right buttons to push, and made me feel incredibly guilty about uprooting her from her life in Colorado and bringing her out to California. She said that if I kicked her out, I would be abandoning her in a place where she knew almost no one, and had nowhere else to turn. I caved in and agreed to give the relationship one more chance.

My alcohol problem was muddying up my perspective in a lot of areas, and it was a self-perpetuating dilemma. I was unhappy because I was drinking, so I drank because I was unhappy. It made perfect sense to me, or would have if I'd realized that was what I was doing. A lot of other areas of my life were in flux as well. Financially, we were barely scraping by from one royalty check to the next, and there was nothing substantial on the musical horizon I could look forward to. Truth is, I hadn't put much effort into pursuing whatever options might have been available to me because I was a little gun shy about projecting too high a profile. There was still the possibility that some of the old Firefall creditors might come looking for me.

When I say 'barely scraping by,' I'm sugar-coating the situation. Between my tax indemnity and the overhead (house payments and such), there was less and less to cover day-to-day expenses with each passing month. It wasn't the best set of circumstances and didn't offer much hope that 'one more chance' would make a a difference.

I know I wasn't showing much backbone about the whole thing and I wish I had, because if I had just told Loretta it was over and she had to leave, I might have spared myself some of the truly unbelievable things that were still to come. Trying to be a nice, honorable guy was soon going to blow up in my face. And I sure as hell didn't know just how bad it was going to get.

The Best Lei'd Plans...

Then one day I got an offer—which I talked myself into believing for the umpteenth time—that might be a game changer for us. It had to do with a mini-tour of small concerts in Hawaii, primarily on the island of Maui. But the tour wasn't how this all started.

It began by virtue of an incredibly unlikely chance occurrence. I was in a bar one afternoon and got to talking with a gentleman and his wife who knew me by virtue of my music. They had a daughter who was going to be married about two weeks from then, and they proposed a trade. They offered me a week in their timeshare condo in Lahaina, Hawaii if I would sing "Just Remember" and "You Are the Woman" at their daughter's upcoming wedding reception in Malibu, California.

It would have been crazy to pass up an offer like that. The thought of a romantic getaway on a tropical South sea island with Loretta healing all our wounds danced in my head, and I went for the deal.

I got my agent to arrange some gigs so I would be able to cover airfare and all the other predictable expenses, plus have a little spending money while we were there. I convinced myself that *maybe* if I took Loretta along and we had a wonderful lover's holiday, we could wipe the slate clean and start over.

I hate to admit it because there were certainly a number of different things involved—the fact that she was an incredible lover was a good incentive—but I had a little voice in my head telling me things any sane person would have recognized as complete idiocy. Things like how a change of scenery would make all the difference. I knew it was a long shot, but I didn't care. I really wanted to believe! And, as far as me being a sane person, I think that ship had long since sailed.

I finalized the contracts for the gigs that had been booked. They weren't exactly big time bookings, but they would be enough to pay the bills and offset any other unforeseen costs during our little vacation. I had long since passed the point of having any ego concerns about whether doing such modest little venues was worthy of my standards and reputation. Grandiose self-delusions are one of the most treacherous and wide spread maladies in the music community. So with high hopes and light hearts, off we went to Hawaii.

If you're ever feeling like the whole world is against you, and you can afford it, go to Hawaii. It's a very hard place to stay depressed. We stayed the first week in the condo, and then moved to a little Travelodge in downtown Lahaina. From those two spots, we drove around the island to my various shows. The shows were widely spaced, time wise, so we had plenty of extra hours to explore a variety of umbrella drinks in between workdays. Just because we had one foot in paradise was no reason to abandon our habits. And overall, we had a good time.

When I say the gigs were modest, I'm not being humble. They were *extremely* modest. One of the shows was in actual fact labeled as a talent show, a detail that the promoter didn't tell me until we got there. He also told me I shouldn't worry about getting paid because all three of the judges were employees of his. The fix was in. And guess who was a deadlock to be the unanimous winner? I don't know if I felt more embarrassed or humiliated by the whole affair. I do know that if I had been awarded a winner's trophy I would have hidden it.

Meanwhile, Loretta was having a great time and we wound up running across a mutual friend of ours named Dennis. Dennis certainly helped make our trip lively. He introduced us to a lot of local friends of his, and we partied a couple of weeks away between my shows. Loretta's temper was behaving itself, and I was almost able to fool myself into believing that the trip had worked its magic. From here on, I just knew things were going to be different.

But my certainty was only a delusion, and by the time we got back to Malibu Lake, I was more confused than ever. On one hand I wanted to believe love would prevail, and on the other hand, I knew it was only a matter of time until Ms. Hyde showed up again. You see, every now and then my sanity would take brief control and a voice would start to whisper in my head that I was an idiot, and hadn't I already seen this movie?

Once again, my optimistic hopes that things had changed were nothing but a foolish delusion. Within a few weeks of getting back to California, all our problems came back in full force. The finances, the lack of work for both of us, and most importantly, the rages.

And it led to exactly the same response from me. More alcohol.

The relationship staggered on for several more months, peppered by several outrageous incidents that would have sent any person in their right mind running for cover. Like the time she made a citizen's arrest on me for beating her up. The police wouldn't do it because it was obvious I had never touched her. And of course I hadn't, so she made the arrest herself. I still ended up spending a night in jail, and I was probably safer there than at home with her.

It went something like this. Loretta launched into one of her furies, and reached for one of my pieces of artwork. I took by her shoulders and sat her down on the couch. Immediately, she screamed at me to stop hitting her and said she was going to call the police. And then she proceeded to make the call. When the two sheriff's deputies arrived, she told them I had been beating her.

The officers looked at her and at the living room where we had been having our disagreement. It was clear they were confused as to why they were there. This was the conversation.

The first cop said, "Ma'am, we don't see any signs of a struggle or any visible marks on you. If you're hurt, please show us where."

Loretta replied, "I don't have any marks, but I'm telling you that he hit me."

"We cannot make an arrest on the basis of your word alone when the visible evidence isn't there," the second cop said.

"There must be something you can do," Loretta said.

The first cop glanced at me with a sympathetic look that said, '*Sorry, pal. I'm required to do this.*'

To her he said, "You could make a citizen's arrest."

"How do I do that?" she asked, her emotions still barely under control.

"Just look him in the eye and say, "I, Loretta_____, arrest you, Rick Roberts

Lame Brain

for assault." This time the cop refused to look at me.

"That's it?" she said.

"That's it."

So that's what she did, and the officers had no choice but to take me with them in their police car. All the way to the police station, I kept asking myself how in the world I had gotten into a crazy situation like this. The answer I got was that the situation wasn't the only thing that was crazy.

Then there was the time she jumped off the third story balcony of the house. She said it was because she was frightened of what I might 'do' to her. Ironically, the scenario was smack in the middle of one of her rages, and I made the mistake of yelling at her, begging her to stop screaming and destroying things. She abruptly went silent, ran out on the balcony, and told me to stay away from her or she'd jump.

With the recent memory of our visit from the police still lingering in my mind, there was no danger of my coming any closer than ten feet to her (and I didn't have a pole), but she continued to warn me off, threatening to jump.

My second mistake was when I said, "I'm not going to get anywhere near you, but come on… You know you're not going to jump." I was wrong. She jumped.

Luckily, she wasn't hurt. The house sat on the side of a hill, and the ground was covered with grass a foot high. So when she made landed, she didn't exactly "hit" the ground. More accurately, her contact simply redirected the angle of her descent. It was like jumping onto a slide.

And then there was the time she hit me with an ax. If that sounds a little far-fetched, believe me, it's true. I have the scar to proof it.

I had locked her out of the house during one of her rages, but she found an ax out in the garage and chopped her way back in to get at me.

The ax incident* was the proverbial last straw. I finally sent her packing.

After all this time, it's gotten a little hard to be sure of the things that took place when we weren't high and which of them happened when we were. But the truth of it is, it really doesn't matter much, because the ongoing reality of addiction cast its shadow on the whole relationship.

---

*You can read about *that* particular event in more detail in my first book, *Song Stories and Other Left-Handed Recollections.*

Rockin' and Rollin' With the Big Boys

Chapter Eight

The next span of time was a little easier to navigate because once Loretta was out of my house, I could concentrate more on revitalizing my career. I was lonely, but no more so than I'd been during the last months of my relationship. My drinking slacked off a bit, primarily because I was no longer walking a twenty-four hour a day tightrope worrying about when the next bombshell would explode around the old hacienda. I'm not saying I got totally sober, since that would certainly not be the truth, but my intake of booze was at least under some degree of control. I had stopped my recent habit of drinking until I was wasted, because there was no longer any need to dull my senses from an unfortunate reality. But just like the old days, I was drinking almost exclusively when I was doing coke, and my cocaine use was generally restricted to when I was at home writing music. And I was doing less of that, too.

I guess it's not entirely true to say that was the only drinking I was doing. I only drank at home when I was writing, but I was a single guy again, and by this time I had learned my way around Malibu. Malibu had two things I found highly desirable. First, it had a lot of upscale restaurant-bars around the beach where I could wile away my lonely afternoons looking out over the beautiful Pacific Ocean. Secondly, there were a lot of lovely women who tended to patronize those bars, and whose acquaintances I hoped to make. So, I had two separate drinking scenarios. The private one and the public one. Fortunately, in the public one, I was always careful not to overindulge because that would have greatly inhibited my second reason for being there—meeting a woman. Even after Loretta, I still hadn't given up hope of finding the right woman.

Eventually, I got fully back into my musical life. I was involved with three long-term musical projects during the '80s, but in the first two of those endeavors—although the level of musicianship was very high—self-discipline was pretty lax.

The first thing I took part in started in the late summer of 1984. One day I got a phone call from an agent who had done a fair amount of booking for Firefall

Lame Brain

in my last days with that band, and he asked me if I was interested in making a three-month commitment to a project he was working on. When I asked him what it was, he told me it was a celebration of one of America's most renowned groups, The Byrds. He said that, considering I had been in The Flying Burrito Brothers with two of the original Byrds' members, I would be a natural for this project.

But I told him I wasn't interested in being part of a tribute band. Why would I? My opinion of tribute bands was that they were for musicians who had no original material to offer, so as an alternative, they become the best at reproducing someone else's work. I have nothing against those guys, since a lot of them are better musicians than I ever was. Such groups always made me think of the old line about "Those who can, do. Those who can't, teach." The agent assured me that wasn't at all what this was going to be.

He told me it was going to be called *"A 20th Anniversary Salute to the Byrds"*, would be strictly legitimate, and was composed of an all-star roster of players. Its members so far included two of the original Byrds, Michael Clarke and Gene Clark, and two members of The Band, Rick Danko and Richard Manuel. Blondie Chaplin, who had been a member of The Beach Boys and later toured with The Rolling Stones, and finally, John York, who was in a later incarnation of The Byrds.

The offer was a very attractive one. It was a dynamite lineup, and they were also planning to have me, Blondie, Richard, and Rick Danko each take a slot in the middle of the show and do a couple of solo numbers from our own catalogues. (A little further down the line, John York would end up doing a solo spot, too.)

My only reservation about the project was how the other members of the original band might feel about it. I didn't know David Crosby that well, having only toured with him the one time. And though I knew Roger McGuinn a little better, I wasn't really in touch with him on a regular basis. So the obvious person to go to for feedback was my friend, Chris Hillman.

Before I agreed to it, I called Chris for his take on the whole thing. His opinion was important to me and he told me to go ahead and do it. We agreed that even if it *was* a tribute band, it was an *all-star* tribute band. And the real test, I figured, would be how well all these first-rate players would sound when we were playing together.

I accepted the offer and flew back to New York for rehearsal with that qualifier in mind. When I got there and we started playing together, it was clear from the first practice that all the guys were pros. I'm not saying that we sounded at all like the original Byrds, because we didn't. But we weren't trying to sound that way.

I know the current definition of a tribute band is a group of guys who can go out and flawlessly reproduce the sound of the artist to whom they are paying homage. But when you have talents on hand like Rick Danko and Richard Manuel, not to mention Blondie, you're going to end up with those people leaving their own stamp on what they are doing.

All three of those guys, as well as Gene and I, were lead vocalists in our own right, and nobody could, or tried to, imitate McGuinn, Crosby, or Hillman's voices. Besides, as I said, it *wasn't* a tribute band. It was a salute to a great group of musicians by a collection of other artists who had achieved successes of their own. So all in all, we actually came more under the heading of a group doing the classic material with our own interpretation coming through. We figured that was okay, because the Byrds didn't sound much like Bob Dylan, either.

The 20th Anniversary Salute band leased a tour bus, and we took off on a tour across the country. There was going to be a surprise in store for all of us, though. As we progressed with the tour, the quality of the band and the response we received from fans pulled us all into a much longer commitment than we had ever anticipated.

Reelin' In the Years

I can't remember most of the gigs we played, because there were so many of them. But there were a few that stood out because of certain unusual things that happened. Even though on the face of it, they may seem like random anecdotes, the connecting factor is that as usual, alcohol was somehow involved in almost all of the events.

There was a time in upstate New York when we were playing in a town near where Rick and Richard lived. When we arrived, Rick and Richard were grabbed by a couple of security men as they stepped off the bus. Evidently, there was for an outstanding warrant from their days with The Band. It was not exactly the homecoming they were expecting.

They managed to dodge going to jail and play the gig, but I'm not sure exactly how. Things on that first tour were a blur most of the time due to a very fast pace, and a reasonably free flow of liquor, pot, and cocaine. When you add that to an equation that started out with a lot of sleep deprivation, long drives, changing time zones, plus the thirty years of time that have elapsed since then, it has a strong fogging effect on the memory.

* * *

Another night that sticks in my mind took place in Aspen. It was still the first version of the Byrds' Salute band and we had finished our show at the Ford Theatre. We had an open day before we had to be in Seattle for our next concert.

Lame Brain

That's better than twelve hundred miles, so our plan was to leave after the show and get to Seattle early on the morning of the gig. By this time it was early winter, and we weren't looking forward to thirty or more hours on the bus, even though we were all planning to spend a lot of time catching up on our sleep.

Somebody at the concert told me that Jeff Hannah and Jimmy Ibbotson from The Nitty Gritty Dirt Band were doing their duo act at a club called Patty Bulgati's in town. Since those guys were longtime friends of mine, I got everyone to agree to let the bus stop at the club just long enough for me to run in and say a brief hello. When we got to the club, I found it was down half a flight of stairs below one of the ski hotels there.

I jumped off the bus and ran inside. The club had two short flights of stairs converging at a big glass picture window with a door on one side. The door was at the back of the room, and when we got in there the place was absolutely packed! Jeff and Jimmy were up at the front on stage.

Those two had a very interesting act, with Jeff standing up, playing guitar and singing, and Jimmy sitting down, playing bass and singing, while using one foot on a bass drum pedal and the other on a high-hat cymbal pedal. There was no way I was going to be able to make my way through the crowd and get up close enough to the stage to yell to them. So I decided to do the next best thing. I raised my hand and waved in hopes one of them would see me.

They were right in the middle of a song when Jeff spotted me, and stopped the song he was playing and immediately went into the chords of my song "Mexico." He motioned at me with his head to come on stage, telling the audience, "Rick Roberts from Firefall is here. Let's bring him up."

The audience parted like the Red Sea. I didn't have much choice but to do it, even though I knew the other guys were waiting outside on the bus. I went up and sang my song with them, but by that time Michael Clarke had either gotten curious or was coming in to hurry me up. Or maybe just to grab a beer for all I know.

When Michael got inside, he saw we were having a good time up there on stage and from his expression, I think he wanted to join in. About then, I realized Jeff was pretty high and Jimmy was smashed. They were indeed having a real good time. The audience was pretty loose too, which was the natural order of things after midnight during ski season.

Jimmy tried to step out on one of those one-foot in diameter tables they have in clubs, and when he lost his balance and started to fall, I managed to catch him and nearly ripped my whole thumbnail off.

When they saw Michael, they motioned for him to come on up on stage, too. He said there was nothing for him to play unless they had a tambourine. They didn't, but Jimmy turned the bass drum over and told Michael to use it like a tom-tom. Then, for reasons of his own which I have never entirely understood, Jimmy laid down on the stage and put his head underneath the bass drum. They started a song that they wanted me to sing lead on, but I didn't know it. After the lead in had stretched on for longer than normal, Jimmy stopped playing bass and lifted the edge of the drum from his neck.

"What's the problem?" he asked.

"I don't know the words to this," I answered.

"No biggie," Jimmy said, and took the microphone.

He put it under the bass drum with him, and sang his heart out to the accompaniment of some very pronounced drum rhythms. The whole scene was getting pretty rowdy and I noticed a couple more of our band had trickled in from the bus. Before long Rick Danko was on stage with us too, clapping his hands and singing without a mike. The crowd was beginning to thin out because it was long after last call, and even though we were still playing, the club people were urging the patrons out.

After he stood back up, Jimmy picked up a chair and threw it through the plate glass window. I thought this was getting a little *too* crazy. We all got off stage and Jeff and Jimmy invited us to come back to the dressing room for some conversation and maybe a sniff. They were using the manager's office for a dressing room, and when we got to the door, it was locked. Jimmy backed off a few steps and said, *"Give me room!"*

A couple of us told him he didn't want to do that, and to just wait a minute for somebody with a key to come. It seemed like he was listening, but then a woman who was standing there with us said, "What's the matter, Jimmy? Ya' chicken?"

That was all it took.

Jimmy got a running start, and the door never had a chance. I'd never seen Jimmy like this before, and I was sure he wasn't one of those guys you come across in some bands who want to destroy everything in sight. Once all this insanity was over, I found out it was all okay. It turned out that this was the club's closing night, and the manager had told Jimmy and Jeff it was no holds barred and that they might as well take out some aggression.

After those events at the club, the ride to Seattle was even more boring.

* * *

One night when we were going on stage at the Cubby Bear in Chicago, I realized I had to go to the bathroom at the last minute. I told the other guys to go ahead and I'd be there before they were tuned up—a matter of sixty seconds. When I came out, they were all up on stage tuning their instruments when I approached from the wings.

Suddenly, I found myself flattened by a big security guy who tackled me and told me I'd have to go back out to the audience because the band was getting ready to play. As soon as my head stopped ringing, I tried to explain to him that

I was *part* of the band, but he didn't believe me. Just then, Gene looked over at us and said, "Rick… Get up here! We're waiting for you!"

I picked myself up, and mumbled something to the guard about how grateful I was to know we were all safe from rogue fans, and went on stage to do the show.

* * *

There was another occasion when a promoter in Nashville was trying to get us to play even though he had never come up with his contracted advance payment. We had been warned this guy might try to stiff us, so the bus driver came up with a novel idea for how to guarantee some payment beforehand. He simply locked up the bus. With all of us on it. And he had neglected to tell us what he was planning to do! He refused to let us off until the promoter came up with the cash. He figured if we weren't able to get off the bus, we wouldn't be doing a show.

Surprising seven musicians with involuntary confinement on a bus is definitely not a good plan, especially when they have just enough liquor and cocaine on hand to magnify the indignity of the situation. And the cross-conversation between us only fueled our feelings of what a rotten deal this was. It may be hard to imagine how these three emotions could happen simultaneously, but as we all sat there, we found ourselves getting progressively more restless, bored, and angry all at the same time! It took about an hour and then the promoter suddenly "found" enough money to pay our guarantee.

I for one would have been happy to give the driver my solemn promise not to go on stage until we were paid, if he would have just *LET ME OFF THE FRIGGIN' BUS!*

Good Things Never Last

After the first six months or so, things began to unravel. As I said before, the whole arrangement was meant to be for one three-month tour only. But we were having such a good time and the audiences liked it so well, the tour just kind of kept on going. It wasn't a nonstop trip and though we'd all gotten to go home on a couple of short breaks, for all intents and purposes, we had been on the road for half a year. Various members of the band had other obligations at home or to another musical situation, and we all needed to take a block of time to recharge our batteries.

In addition, the original enthusiasm of the promoters had slacked off a trifle and the venues were not quite as first rate as they had been to start with, nor the paydays quite as lucrative. That may have had something to do with the fact that, starting out, the money men perceived the chance to book us as a onetime offer, and when we continued to play more shows the exclusivity factor was lost. That meant we weren't able to ask quite as hefty a price, which in turn meant that the budget started to be a consideration, and we had to start economizing the operation.

Something else was happening that took a little of the magic away. When we showed up at venues now the marquee advertised us not as "A 20th Anniversary Salute to the Byrds" but simply as "A Salute to the Byrds," which was reasonable I guess since we'd outlasted the 20th anniversary. But it did make us sound a lot more like a tribute band.

I think we all thought that the name recognition factor of the band personnel would serve as a counterbalance, but either the promoters weren't emphasizing that enough or our names didn't make that big of a difference to people anymore. One way or another, the message we were getting from our agents was that the band was no longer such an easy sell to the concert bookers. Naturally, the band wanted to believe the problem was the promoters not pitching it right, but in our hearts we knew how quickly fame can slip away. We all had to face the fact that our former glories might be yesterday's news.

The real muttering started one night when we arrived at our gig and were being billed as "The New Byrds." None of us had signed up for that!

A couple of us complained to the agent, and to Michael and Gene. The explanation we got was that the billboard wasn't big enough to fit the whole title. We grudgingly accepted that even when it happened the next night, too. It definitely felt uncomfortable for several of us. At the time, though, I think we wanted to believe that explanation so we didn't question things too carefully.

But then one night we drove up to the venue and read what was written on the marquee. "Tonight Only: The New Byrds, featuring Gene Clark, Michael Clarke, Rick Danko, Richard Manuel, Rick Roberts, etc." That made it crystal clear that it wasn't a matter of fitting the name on a billboard. It was just a cynical way to market the band. Those of us who had never been Byrds hit the roof. We thought it stunk to try to put something over on the audiences that way and think the band wouldn't notice to boot!

Several alternative names were soon offered. I remember suggesting we call the group "Phoenix" after the mythical bird that rose from its own ashes. I was told there was probably already a band with that name, and also that if we called ourselves that, *it would make it harder to book the band!* So a new name didn't happen, but we did finally get everyone involved with the booking process to meet us halfway. We'd agree to go back to calling us "A Salute to the Byrds," but another bit of what had made our group so special was lost.

Richard Manuel was the first to leave, partly because of the growing number of compromises, and partly because of some troubles at home. That was a huge disappointment, not only because of his talent, but also because Richard was one of the funniest men I have ever had the pleasure of working with or knowing. He had a completely deadpan delivery no matter what he was saying. He reminded me of the comedian Steven Wright who never even cracks a smile while his audience could be rolling on the floor laughing. Richard made every bus trip something to look forward to.

We kept the band going by replacing Richard with Nicky Hopkins, which was obviously not a step down in talent. Nicky didn't have as big a name on the street, but he had played with just about every major band that ever came out of England. (I did some research, and found that among his performance credits, he could list The Beatles, The Rolling Stones, and The Who, just to name a few.) He also had several solo albums. He was a very soft spoken and laid back Englishman with that wry sense of British humor, so we didn't lose much in the levity department, either.

Having seen the first cracks in the unity of the band, we knew it wouldn't be long before other members started to make their exits. With that in mind, the camaraderie that was responsible for making the whole thing so much fun began to slip away.

Ricky D. left shortly after Richard, another big letdown. He was a fine bass player, and always had an inexhaustible reserve of energy, as well as a huge heart. Sometimes he'd have his face about two inches from yours, talking so fast it felt like you were standing in front of a human hurricane that was going to blow you over any minute. Ricky was truly a great guy. He had an abundance of love for others, and was one of the most sensitive people I ever worked with. I don't have any recollection of him ever saying anything bad about anybody who hadn't earned a whole lot worse than just a bad word.

When he left, he said he needed to take a rest and spend more time with his family. It was only a few years after that (1989) when his son Eli died at the age of seventeen of asphyxiation due to a bout of heavy drinking. It broke Ricky's heart, and even though he lived for another ten years and moderated his lifestyle, he seemed somehow diminished after Eli's death. A little of the spark had gone out of him.

Sometime shortly after Ricky left, Blondie decided to go, and soon afterwards Nicky called it a day, too. We replaced Blondie with Billy Darnell, a very solid guitarist from L.A. who had previously worked with Roger McGuinn for a while. Finally, the only remaining members from the group that started out were Gene, Michael, John, and me.

By this juncture, the band had gone seriously downhill financially. We had long since given up our tour bus, and the places we were playing were mostly clubs and small auditoriums. By the last days we were touring in a motor home that Michael's wife had put on her credit card. Things were getting pretty frayed around the edges. There was even an interlude in the fall of 1985 when Gene was staying in his hotel room all day, every day, drinking so much he had become an embarrassment on stage. We had to send him home to California for a week to straighten out while we did shows without him.

As I look back at those years, I realize I should have taken my leave long before I did. But once again, my musical future when I parted company with the band would be a blank page and I was nervous to about walking into such an uncertain future. I also believe that as the years go by and the affiliations accumulate, it gets harder and harder to walk away from people and a band you've grown accustomed to, even when it should be obvious things are deteriorating.

There was also my sense of loyalty to Michael after all the different situations we had shared together. Michael and I had been together for most of the time since I first became a recording artist. He was the first one to take me under his wing when I joined The Flying Burrito Brothers. I remember going to The Troubador, a legendary hangout for rock and rollers, after my very first rehearsal with the band. Even though my fate with the group was far from being secured, Michael was already introducing me to all these famous people as "Rick Roberts, our new singer." We did the four most successful Firefall albums together, and here we were in our third career hookup. Things like that are hard to just walk away from.

And, in spite of all the personnel changes, I wasn't truly aware that the band was on the wane. It's easy to fool yourself, because the decline sort of sneaks up on you without you noticing on a day-to-day basis. It's only when you stop and look at the bigger picture that you realize how far you've dropped. Besides, even at the end it was still a good band with some very good players.

Our last bass player was Carlos Bernal, and he had been our road manager before he became part of the band. That's not as bad as it looks in writing because he was a pretty fair bass player, and had done the same thing, changing from roadie to bass player in one of the last lineups of the real Byrds, when Chris Hillman was still with the band.

On that particular occasion (as it was told to me), The Byrds were in the middle of a world tour. When it came time for them to leave England for South Africa, Gram Parsons refused to go, so Chris had to change from bass to guitar, and Carlos took over on bass. When the Salute band started putting two guys to a room to save money, Carlos and I ended up together. He was a good roommate except for dominating the bathroom.

When I did some checking on dates, I realized I had stayed with the band even longer than I thought. One particular event that I could isolate in time proved it to me. It happened one morning when I was in Toronto. Just before checkout time at the hotel, I was watching the launch of one of our space shuttles on TV while Carlos was in the bathroom. The date was January 28, 1986. The shuttle was the Challenger. One moment it was rising majestically into the morning

Lame Brain

sky, and then suddenly it was nothing but a big noise and a bright flash of colors and flames. I remember it all too well.

The group had a rather curious dynamic during its lifetime. Our success level was going backwards, at least in terms of the trappings that normally defined success. We started off with our own tour bus and lodgings at the very best hotels. Our concerts were in large, high profile venues, and we were all making pretty impressive money. By the time I left the group, we were making about four hundred a week apiece and staying at little roadside motels where the TVs were bolted to the table. And the rooms seldom had any cable service, either.

In spite of all the changes that took place, both in personnel and finances, I have to admit that those were some of my most wonderful years. In a way, having to scramble to make ends meet was almost like a trip down memory lane. We had all been in some band or other that had experienced this stage of building a career in the music biz. It was kind of strange having it happen in reverse though, where you start off in nice big venues and traveling in style, and then work your way down the ladder.

The bittersweet aspect of looking back at that marvelous group of people is to know that so many of them are now gone. If you count Nicky Hopkins, since he joined when it was still almost the original makeup, five of the eight people have said their final goodbyes, all of them much too soon, and I miss them all very much. Michael Clarke, Gene Clark, Rick Danko, Richard Manuel, and Nicky Hopkins…

Even though only Gene and Michael died directly from substance abuse, all those guys I toured with except Nicky were pushing it pretty hard all the time, and I was right there running neck and neck with them. Not surprisingly, the only two surviving members of that band besides me are Blondie Chaplin and John York, who both kept their partying to a minimum.

I've had quite a while to think about it all since then, and I've often wondered why some of us in music are such easy prey for alcohol and drugs, while others never seem to fall into the many traps that are always there. Never mind all the various influences that every person has to contend with in life. I'm just talking about the things directly related to the music world. John York did a lot of his work as both a studio musician and an addition to already established bands. Blondie Chaplin came to the states with a South African band called The Flame, but soon began to work doing sessions and ultimately joining numerous other groups. The same goes for Nicky Hopkins. They all had a chance to see a lot of different players up close who had already locked in to their various lifestyles.

Meanwhile, Danko, Manuel, Clark, and Clarke all hit the big time with the guys they had been playing with for a while, and only got the benefit of observing that one set of folks. Certainly, Blondie, John, and Nicky showed character in their choices, but I think consideration should be given to the fact that they probably had a more complete education by virtue of observation.

That may have afforded them a better perspective on things. And I certainly don't think the other guys lacked character.

* * *

During my tenure with those guys, the 'just getting by' thing finally ran out its string and I lost my house to foreclosure. But surprisingly enough, that was when I fell into one of the neatest situations I have ever been lucky enough to find. I acquired a roommate who wasn't really a roommate. And to give credit where credit is due, it was Loretta who introduced us. She had a friend named Dean who was a professional football place kicker. He was looking for someone to share the rent on his big condo up north of Malibu. The nifty thing was that he was away half the time at training camp and other football activities, and I was away the rest of the time playing with the Salute band. So we both got twice the space *and* our privacy for half the price. We got to be close friends and when we eventually moved out of that place after our lease expired and the rent went way up, we partnered up at another spot in Malibu proper. That place was too small, so we found a little horse ranch up in the mountains behind town and they rented us two cabins, one at either end of the ranch. Somewhere in the midst of those different addresses, I realized the Salute band had pretty much had its run, so I took my leave.

Overall, I was feeling pretty good about how things were going. The only bad news was that once again, I had a lot of time on my hands and only knew of one way to spend it. I went back to haunting the bars in Malibu, still looking for love. Eventually, Dean found the right woman and moved in with her and I found the ranch to be a little too isolated without a friend around, so I moved again.

I relocated down to Hermosa Beach, one of the Pacific Ocean communities on the southern end of the L.A. basin. I felt it was my duty to familiarize myself with a whole new set of beachfront bars in my ongoing search for someone to share my life. Obviously, the bars were not the best place to find anything more than a one night affair, but I was kind of short on friends and options. This was yet another new place, and I'd been out on the road so much the time that I hadn't built many close relationships.

I did have one good buddy named Dan Dugan, who was a bachelor like me. We'd gotten to know one another when we both lived in Malibu, and he had moved south a little while before I did. He was one town up, in Manhattan Beach. We hit the bars together for a while and then he too found the right woman and I was a on my own again. He did leave me a small going away gift though. When he moved in with his girlfriend, he bequeathed his ocean view apartment in Manhattan Beach to me.

In and of itself, that was a nice thing. But I still had a few things to do. Being

Lame Brain

in a good apartment with a great view didn't get me any closer to satisfying my musical urges. The Salute Band had been a fun way to spend some time, but it didn't provide me with an outlet for my own music. I hadn't had that since I left my last band in Colorado.

New Horizons

Chapter Nine

By that time, I had outlasted most of my fears of any Firefall creditors coming after me for outstanding band debts behind me, and felt good to go full-speed ahead with my postponed musical plans. So I started my search for players to form a new band. This would become my second long-term commitment of the '80s. With a music scene like L.A. had at that time, I figured my best bet was to go out to the numerous clubs that flourished in the beach towns, keep my eyes and ears open, and see what developed. Also, I still banked in Malibu and got my haircuts from a woman named Lari White up there, so I also scouted the places in that area whenever I was in the vicinity.

There were top flight players all over the place, if you just paid attention. It was like Boulder in the '70s minus the altitude. And just to cover all my bases, I put the word out to a few friends to be on the lookout for any musicians whose chops particularly impressed them.

I got lucky early on and happened to see a guy named Bray Ghiglia playing guitar, keyboards, and singing as a solo act. He was playing at an old hangout of mine from my Malibu Lake days, in a great indoor-outdoor place in Calabasas called the Sagebrush Cantina—a wonderful spot to spend the afternoon drinking and looking at pretty women.

I approached him and told him who I was, mentioning that I was thinking of forming a band. And would he be interested?

He told me he'd like to check it out, and asked me who else was involved.

I told him I was just starting to get things organized, and he had just received my first invitation.

Bray was a long time local and knew a lot of people, and he thought he might be able to help recruit some other top-notch players. I then found out he also played sax and flute. And that's one reason I said I was lucky, because having someone who can play all those instruments can make a world of difference in what a band can do. Especially when they can play them well.

That was the jumping off point, because just like when I hooked up with Jock

Lame Brain

and it led to forming Firefall, I now had a tangible base to build upon.

We started off with Billy Darnell (whom I knew from the Salute band) on lead guitar and Mark Andes sitting in on bass. There was a drummer that Bray knew named Lynn Coulter who filled things out and gave us a unit to work with so we could start rehearsing. Mark was just temporary. He was a full-time member of Heart at that time, and was helping out while they were on a break until we found the right guy to be our permanent bass player.

After we did a few rehearsals together, we went out to a Japanese restaurant one night when practice was finished. Mark told us then he couldn't rehearse with us anymore. He said he was leaving town to start a new round of work with Heart.

Once again, God must have been smiling on me, because a few booths away, Randy Meisner was having dinner. I knew he had left the Eagles, and I hadn't heard of him being involved with anything else.

I had known Randy for years, what with him playing and singing on my first solo album, as well as him being a frequent guest at a poker game I was in with Don Henley and Glenn Frey during the early '70s, and just from running into one another occasionally. It was obvious that if he *was* interested, he would be a wonderful addition to my group.

Immediately, I went over and struck up a conversation and asked him what he was doing currently. I told him I was putting a new band together and was looking for a bass player. To my surprise and great pleasure, he was interested in knowing more about the idea. And just for good measure, his lunch partner that day was Dewey Martin, the original drummer from Buffalo Springfield. Dewey asked if I might need a drummer, too. That sounded like a pretty powerful lineup to me. I think I've mentioned before, Buffalo Springfield has always been one of my all-time favorite bands. So I told Dewey we could definitely give it a try, but as a result, I'm afraid Lynn Coulter never really had a fair chance.

Now that the personnel were shaping up, we needed a name. So, we christened ourselves Rick Roberts and Open Secret. The players were: Dewey on drums, Randy on bass and vocals, Billy on guitar, me on guitar and vocals, and Bray on a multitude of instruments and vocals.

Ironically, Billy had stayed on with the Salute to the Byrds band after I left and was still traveling with them. Although by now, they were just calling themselves The New Byrds, and were not working full time. I don't know for sure who else was involved with that, but he felt he didn't have time to do both jobs so he chose to go on with them. We parted on good terms and Dewey suggested a guitar player, Cary Park, to take over for Billy.

We gave Cary an audition, and he was exactly what we were looking for. With newfound confidence, we did a few gigs with the Open Secret name, and hired my old agent pal named Geoff Blumenauer to book us.

It didn't take us long to realize we were wasting a major weapon in our arsenal by not having Randy's name featured more prominently in some way. Having been one of the original Eagles and the composer of some of their best-known songs, including "Take It to the Limit," Randy wasn't someone we should be hiding. So we changed the name to the Roberts-Meisner Band, and immediately saw results in the form of a lot more bookings.

The group got along better than most other bands I had been with, and that made touring a lot more comfortable. But there was still something that didn't feel right; one thing that was out of step. Somehow or other, the drums never quite fit with the rest of what was being played. I don't know exactly how to describe it. Dewey was a good drummer, but somehow the grooves just never quite settled in.

Dewey himself was also a little out of sync with everyone else. He was a nice man with a big heart, but he was marching to a different drummer, if you'll forgive the pun. He frequently did rather strange things that the band came to refer to as "Deweyisms." He let us know he was on a strict regimen of vitamins, and he persisted in taking large doses of niacin just before going to bed at night. This had a very noticeable effect on his complexion. When we were out on the road, he'd come out of his hotel room and his skin would be glowing bright orange.

Once when we were driving between two venues I was reading a new book as we went into a dark tunnel. I just kept on reading because I was sitting next to Dewey. Ha, ha. Okay, I just made that up, but he *was* often luminescent for a couple of hours.

There were various types of activities that came under the heading of Deweyisms.

One day as we were driving through the mountains of eastern Washington, en route from Post Falls, Idaho to Seattle. Dewey announced he had to take a leak and he couldn't wait. So, we got off at the next exit, which was in the middle of nowhere. There were no gas stations or other facilities, so we pulled off to the side of the road. There were hills full of evergreens on both sides of the road, and we invited Dewey to step outside and relieve himself.

He got out of the vehicle and ran up into the forest, for a little privacy I suppose, while the rest of us waited in the van and made small talk. Five minutes passed and Dewey still wasn't back. He seemed to be taking a long time to answer the call of nature. So I looked up the hill and saw that he was wandering around, as if he hadn't decided which tree he should irrigate. I yelled at him to hurry up, and before long he arrived back at the van. He was very excited when he got in, and said, *"Hey Rick. Look at this."* And he handed me a pine cone.

Since the whole hill was littered with pinecones, I expected that this one must have silver caps on all the little tip ends or something. No such luck. It was just your everyday run-of-the-mill pinecone.

I told him it was very nice and handed it back to him. He looked at it again

Lame Brain

briefly without saying a word and threw it out.

There were a lot more incidents, but basically, they were all just Deweyisms. He had, like many of us, been through the whole drug and alcohol scene, including the really hard drugs. To his credit, he had cleaned up his act completely and was now totally drug and alcohol free. He had also recently established a full-fledged relationship with God, and as with many newly born-again people, much of his conversation centered on his new-found faith.

None of us had a problem with his faith, but for the sake of the band's sound, we decided we needed to make a change. It was not because of the Deweyisms or his religious conversations, or because we had fun with his little quirks. It was simply that we weren't all on the same page musically.

Once I knew what we needed to do, the next thing was to figure out who to get to replace him. That turned out not to be a problem, because the man for the job had already been coming to some of our shows and watching what we did. His name was Ron Grinel, and he had been the drummer for the Souther-Hillman-Furay band, and Dan Fogelberg's group, among others. When we talked to Ron about the change, he told us he would love to join.

But everybody in the band liked Dewey, and no one felt comfortable just cutting him loose without some kind of bonus, or severance pay, or something. As it turned out, we snagged a booking that would make our parting a little more humane. It was a gig playing Harrah's in Reno for two weeks with a nice fat paycheck at the end, so at least we could send him on his way with a few dollars in his pocket.

It's somewhere around 500 miles from Los Angeles to Reno, and since we were going to be there for two full weeks, everyone decided to drive their own cars. We wanted to have transportation available for any side trips we chose to take en route, as well as being able to get around while we were there. I thought it would be better if Dewey wasn't made aware of the coming change until after our engagement, because it might have an adverse effect on his performance. We didn't have any work scheduled for a while after Reno, so he would still be getting proper notice and he wouldn't be losing out on any promised money.

So the plan was that we would do the shows, go home, and then Randy and I would take Dewey out to lunch and tell him we were going to try something else. That seemed like the cleanest way to make the break.

We did the shows, and they went well. The only uncomfortable thing that happened was that Dewey proposed we rename the band The Roberts-Meisner-Martin Band. I told him that was kind of unwieldy and would never fit on his drumhead. So, instead, he went out and got the words DEWEY MARTIN printed in big white block letters on the black drumhead.

Our road manager at the time, Darrell Gray, saw a great opportunity in that. As he read it, Dewey was decorating his drumhead as a protest about not getting to have his name added to the group name. Darrell perceived it as a childish display of pique, so he decided he would add a little decoration of his own.

The night after Dewey showed up with his monogrammed drum, Darrell went up before the show with some color-coordinated duct tape and covered the "D" in Dewey, so that the drum now proudly identified our drummer as EWEY MARTIN. Having seen that, it seems to me it's kind of a shame Dewey didn't spell his name "DOOWHEE".

Everyone made their own arrangements for when they planned to make the drive back home, and I told them I would call to schedule rehearsal in a week or so.

I left early the next morning and drove all day back to my place in Hermosa Beach. I got home sometime in the middle of the evening and went right to bed. About 2 A.M. the phone rang, and it was Dewey.

I braced myself for another of his off-the-wall ideas (a fairly frequent occurrence), but that was not what he was calling for. He wanted to borrow money. I couldn't believe he'd be calling for money in the middle of the night, and especially when I'd just paid him a bundle the night before. Then he told me his story.

Dewey drove a big, white classic Cadillac (circa 1965 or so), and he told me when he was just outside Palmdale, one of the easternmost suburbs of L.A., his rear axle fell off. I tried not to laugh, because I could picture it so clearly in my mind. This big old white honker Cadillac sliding down the Interstate with its ass end dragging and sparks flying everywhere. And when he tried to put the brakes on, nothing!

Meanwhile, coming up from behind him, were the two back wheels still connected by their axle and slowly rolling past the driver's side of the car, as he came to a stop in the middle of the highway. He brought me back to reality by telling me the estimated cost, and how that plus towing and a motel room for the night were going to eat his pay plus a bit more.

I got his information and promised to wire him $500 first thing in the morning when Western Union opened. It took him a day or so to get his car back and complete his trip, but he still had another surprise waiting for him in L.A.

He was living in Topanga Canyon at the time with his two beloved dogs. When he got home, there was yellow police tape all over his yard. It seems his house was a crime scene. What had happened was Dewey had hired an acquaintance from rehab to watch his place and take care of his dogs while he was in Nevada. The friend was an ex-junkie who got Dewey to pay him in advance so he had money to buy dog food and such.

It turned out the ex-junkie was not completely an *EX*-junkie. The guy was being given a perfect opportunity to get high just once more, for old time's sake. So evidently, he went out and scored, went into the bathroom where there were no windows, shot up, and OD'ed!

After what must have been a few days, the neighbors called the authorities to make a complaint about a very unsavory odor emanating from Dewey's house. The police came to investigate, ended up having to break into the house, and discovered the body. They took the two dogs to the pound, and cordoned off the house. This was the scene Dewey came home to. *Welcome back!*

Randy and I took him to lunch two days later and fired him. I know it sounds cold-hearted, but we had to realize that the two situations were not connected, and there was no legitimate way to keep him in the band simply because we felt bad about his misfortune.

On the upside, he did get his dogs back, and they had probably been better cared for than they would have been by his pal.

That was the last time I saw Dewey, but I did try to keep track of what he was doing. I know that shortly his departure from the band, he took a job as a chauffeur for a Christian limousine service, but then I lost track of him.

The Changing of the Guard

Chapter Ten

We didn't take much of a hiatus while we were switching drummers. Just as we had planned, we replaced Dewey with Ron Grinel, and that put some fresh energy into the band.

Ron is a very smart man, and a full-fledged go-getter. He invited us to move the rehearsals over to his house, and we went to work on new material, as well as polishing up our entire repertoire. Right from the start it felt like a more natural fit, and whether by virtue or simply by coincidence, we started getting a lot more work. That was all right by me, because gigs had been getting a little less frequent and paying a $500 a man retainer every week off the road was becoming pretty expensive.

By this time, it had been over five years with no legal repercussions from my Firefall creditors, so that had ceased to be a concern for me. I've mentioned before that it was still a faint shadow in the back of my mind, and probably remained as such until the statute of limitations ran out, whenever that was. But it was no longer a primary component in my ongoing plans. Now that I had, for all intents and purposes, ceased to worry about it, the process of searching for a record deal began.

We went into the studio and cut at least a half a dozen tunes, making sure we maintained a high level of quality. We had a first-class engineer, Steve Strassman, who had worked with a number of top artists like Paul Simon and people in that bracket.

One day when I remarked to him on what exceptionally good demos he was making, he said, *"Rick, you know me. I don't make demos…I make records."*

And by the way, if that sounds arrogant, trust me, it was nothing of the sort. It was a simple statement of truth. What Steve was saying was he put just as much effort into what we were doing, as if it were going to be pressed to vinyl (they still made records back then) straight from the studio.

John Stronach was the nominal producer, but most of our arrangements were a result of our live renditions of the songs. This is not to diminish John's skills.

Lame Brain

At the demo stage, a lot of the fine-tuning a producer does is still in the planning stages, to be implemented into the final product.

I had been writing quite a bit again, and Bray and Cary were also writing some, so we had a lot of material to pick from. Randy was in a bit of a dry spell—rare for him, as he was an accomplished pro. I knew from personal experience that even the most dependable and consistent composers have non-productive periods. I was confident that when the spirit moved him, Randy would show up one day with a killer new song.

My preference has always been to have more than one contributing songwriter in a band. That way, you give the group additional dimensions, showcase different sensibilities, and more often than not, a sort of subconscious competitive spirit develops. Everybody seems to stimulate one another, and each composer tries to make sure his songs measure up to everyone else's.

The band was excellent, and I (with a couple of contributions from Cary and Bray) had written a healthy amount of strong new material for us. However, when we went looking for a record deal, there were no immediate takers. There was less excitement than we had hoped for, and to be honest, with the track records of some of us, less than we had expected.

At the time, we were sure the main reason was that the music industry was in the midst of a major transformation. The West Coast sound that both Randy (with the Eagles) and I (with Firefall) had been closely associated with had survived the disco era, but rap and hip-hop were starting to dominate the charts. We thought our difficulties in drawing interest was because nobody was willing to take a chance on a band with a sound that might be yesterday's news.

Actually, it may well have been more our "track records" that were hanging things up. I think that both Randy and I, besides having the two most successful backgrounds, may also have acquired a reputation around the business for being big-time party guys. Once again, even when drinking didn't directly impact the situation, the consequences remained and indirectly ambushed matters with a ripple effect.

In our live shows, we had the luxury of choosing to do as much of any set as we wanted, using hit songs that either Randy or I had written and/or recorded. In actuality, we tried to mix those songs in equally with new material. That way, the audience could relate to us as artists they were familiar with hearing, but still have the feeling of being exposed to something new. Whatever got the audience going was okay by us.

We had a great time playing all over the country back in the days when you didn't get to just buy a Pro Tools rig and make your own record. In case you're not familiar with what Pro Tools is, it's a digital recording device that you can set up in your garage and do studio quality recording. All for a very nominal price, which makes doing a CD possible for almost anybody.

In case my feelings didn't come across in my choice of words, I have mixed emotions about the ready availability of recording these days. To put it briefly, the good news is that anybody can make a CD. The bad news is that *anybody* can make a CD. In the old days, some really worthy artists slipped through the cracks because for some reason or another, they didn't excite the record companies. That was a bad thing and should no longer be a problem with today's technology. But on the other side of it, there are some folks around who should restrict their playing to their living rooms and their singing to the shower. At least the record companies served as a filter so that artists whose music deserved to be heard didn't get swallowed by a glut of worthless pap. The easy accessibility of high quality recording gear has literally changed the face of music. Recently, finding the good stuff is like looking for the proverbial needle. It's enough to drive a man to drink! Of course, that's just my opinion.

Distractions From the Inevitable

The next year and a half were devoted to that same familiar rhythm. Go out on tour for anywhere from a few days to a week. Take a few days off. Spend a couple of weeks in rehearsal. Repeat cycle.

As with every band that goes out on the road, we had certain nights when things didn't go quite the way we planned. And naturally, those are the gigs that linger in my memory long after the smooth nights have faded away.

One night we were playing at a resort hotel on the coast of Oregon. When we went up on stage for the first of two shows, we noticed during the very first song the sound was really different from the way it had been at our sound check. We asked the soundman what he had changed, and could he put things back the way they had been earlier? He spoke over the house PA and said nothing was different; we were imagining things. Which seemed a little rude to me, but we were more interested in getting the sound straightened out than bridling at insults.

I think both Randy and I said at the very same time that something was *not at all the same*. Cary jumped in and agreed with us. He told the guy it was definitely different than what it had been before, and maybe it was *his* imagination or *his* ears.

The soundman flipped Cary off, shouted to us that we could get screwed, and added a few choice words concerning our mothers as well as the circumstances of our births. Then he cranked the levels on the sound board to maximum and walked out. Suddenly everyone in sight tried to cover their ears as the room was filled with an ear-splitting burst of feedback.

After a moment of confusion and extreme auditory pain, our road guy, Darrell Grey, got behind the board and turned it down so the screeching stopped. He did

Lame Brain

some quick equalizing, and managed to give us a reasonable sound mix, so we went back to work.

About three songs into the set, a young woman came up to the front of the stage right in the middle of a tune, and yanked on Randy's pants. The stage was only raised about three feet from the main floor so he was within reach. He was singing at the time, and he tried to signal her to wait until the end of the song.

She ignored the signals, and kept on yanking.

Finally, Randy stopped and looked down at her and yelled, *"WHAT DO YOU WANT?!"*

"Could I have your autograph?" she asked timidly.

At that point, Ron called me over, and said, *"Do you know what I'm going to do between sets?"*

I told him I didn't know, and he said, *"I don't know either, exactly, but it will be something involving a large quantity of tequila."*

It had been a long night and we were all tired, so all I could do was nod and say, *"Count me in!"*

* * *

Then there was the evening when we were performing on "Nashville Now", hosted by Mr. Ralph Emory, a delightful but somewhat older gentleman. Before the band played, Ralph had Randy and I sit for a brief interview.

I know Ralph had a handle on his country music, but for our little give and take, he was pretty locked in to his scripted notes. I had to curb the urge to shoot him some totally off the wall answer to one of his stock questions. But I wasn't sure where that might lead, and sometimes it's better just to leave well enough alone. So I kept quiet.

Anyway, the way they had set up the bandstand on stage was in three levels. On the first level in front were Randy and me. On the second level were Bray and his keyboards, and Cary on guitar. On the third and highest level was Ron, sitting behind his drum set. We were doing two songs, the first of which was my song, *"You Are the Woman,"* and the second of which was Randy's song "Take It to The Limit".

The way it was scripted, we would do the songs and then the show would go to commercial. During the commercial, the band would leave the stage and the stage crew would break down the set. Everything on those TV shows runs on a split second time schedule, so when we finished our second song, the crew was waiting.

Ron stood up from his drum stool to shake Cary's hand. The crew thought he was getting up to go, so when Ron sat back down there was no longer a drum stool there. They had already grabbed it. Ron fell directly backwards into about eight feet of empty air before landing on his back on the tile floor.

Initially, the "Nashville Now" people were very concerned about him, and promised to cover any medical costs. As time went by, and the situation was resolving itself, they stalled, trying to deny any responsibility. I think they hoped Ron would just fade away. When I spoke with him about it during that limbo period, he said, *"I guess they don't realize they're dealing with a hungry little Jew here, and I ain't going nowhere!"*

The next night we had been booked to play at the Bluebird Cafe, and in order to do the show, we had to prop Ron up against the wall so he could play through the pain. In the long term, the whole mess ended up in court. Ron was not permitted to hire a California lawyer, but was restricted to being represented by a jurisdictional advocate. In other words, a lawyer from Nashville. He hired Tyree Harris, generally considered to be the dean of the area legal folk.

After all, in going against "Nashville Now," he was taking on not just them, but also the parent company—who were major league corporate big business—for the show. Just to give you an idea of how serious the whole business ended up being, the case dragged out for so long that Mr. Harris actually developed dementia and had to abandon the case before things were resolved. Because of that, the legal process had to start all over, with Ron engaging a new lawyer.

Things were finally worked out with Ron eventually receiving a settlement from the show. When I spoke to him, he told me that by the time he had paid all his legal fees, doctor bills, and expenses (air travel, hotel bills, etc.) he had about enough left over for a six pack of beer, domestic of course.

I know he still suffers from residual back pain, and he finally gave up playing drums as his primary pursuit to take a position with Rick Springfield's touring operation. He still plays some, but no longer full time.

* * *

One of the more entertaining sequences took place in Atlantic City, where we were playing at Harrah's Casino for two weeks. For whatever reason, the promoters at the hotel had only been willing to spring for one room at the hotel for the band, so we let Randy have it since he had brought Lana, his girlfriend and future wife.

The rest of us decided we'd rather not be on the strip, and booked rooms at a nice, little hotel about twenty five miles outside of town. Our schedule called for two shows a night Sunday through Thursday and three shows on Friday and Saturday. The hardest part was not having a room to go to during the three hours between shows.

I personally read a lot, drank steadily, and played the poker machines. I did happen to hit a royal flush one night for $1,500 but the time between shows still went by at a snail's pace.

One night, Randy suggested we go out to a wine store a block or so from the

Lame Brain

hotel. They had quality wine at good prices, which is not that easy to find at a casino. Wine, yes. Quality, no.

We thought we'd share a bottle between sets, and bought three. I guess Randy drank a bottle by himself between the time we bought it and the second show.

When we went back on stage, we did one song before Randy took off his bass and handed it to me. He said, "I can't do this right now." Then he walked off stage and left us to wing it the rest of the way through the show with Cary playing bass.

When we were finished, we saw Lana. I asked her how Randy was.

Lana looked confused and replied, *"Forget HOW is Randy. I'd rather know WHERE is Randy?"*

We told her we thought he went to his room, but she hadn't seen him. We finally solved the mystery about an hour later when we found him peacefully sleeping in the corner booth of the bar next to the showroom. The whole episode was not anything like Randy's normal behavior. It says a lot about having so much time between turning it on when you go on stage, then turning it off when you come off, then killing two or three hours before you have to do the exact same thing again. Multiply that by two weeks, and it gets pretty disorienting, as well as mind-numbingly boring. And unfortunately, it's a great excuse to drink every night.

* * *

In May of 1988, we were booked for two nights at Calamity Jane's, a new club in Las Vegas. Jane was a great lady and a former L.V. working girl, who had changed her job to that of overseeing others in her profession. We were staying at the Showboat Hotel and Casino on the outskirts of Las Vegas which happened to be right across the street from Calamity's. Jane was paying us an outrageous amount for the shows, and when I questioned her about how she could afford it, she said, "Don't worry about it. If I lose too much on you guys, I'll just send out a few more girls."

On the morning we were checking out of the hotel to go home, I got up and opened my curtains. We all had rooms on the 17th floor, so I could see several miles out over the desert. I looked outside at the overcast sky made up of those light gray, not quite white clouds. I knew there was a PGA tournament going on in the area, and someone had recently told me only white balls are permissible in PGA golf tournament play. I remember thinking how I'd hate to be hitting a white ball into that sky.

Suddenly, right in the center of my vision, there was a huge ball of fire from what looked like a very big explosion. The flames were obviously coming from something chemical or metallic, because they were shooting up in shades of blue and green. I knew the airport was in that direction with my first thought being that a plane had crashed, but the blaze seemed too big to be a plane.

As I was standing there wondering just what it could be, the shock wave hit the hotel. I was knocked off my feet and down onto my bed. I got off the bed and ran out into the hall where I was already beginning to hear the sounds of confused and puzzled voices. There were a lot of people milling around in the hallway, including some of the band, all looking confused and frightened.

"Did you see that? Come here, I'll show you!" I said to the guys and went back into my room. I was followed not only by my guys, but also a teenaged boy and an elderly couple in their seventies. I explained what I had seen and pointed to the flames when suddenly there was a second explosion.

The elderly lady asked me what we should do, and I told her I recommended sitting down. Sure enough, after about thirty seconds, the hotel rocked again with the second shock wave. I'm glad the old couple had sat down, because they would surely have been knocked down otherwise.

I later found out that all the people in the gambling area where there were no windows thought that the "big one" had finally hit L.A. Since we had been scheduled to fly out that morning, I was already packed, so I grabbed my bag and told my guys to get theirs, so we could get out of there.

When we went back out into the hall, Randy was standing there with his bags. I said to him to come on, and we'd get on the elevator. Randy said there was no way he was getting on any elevator with the hotel shaking around like it was, and he was taking the stairs. 17th floor, remember.

When we got down to the lobby and the elevator doors opened, I stepped out. I was just in time to see the door to the stairwell fly open as a panting, red-faced Randy lurched out with a suitcase in each hand. All I could do was gently inquire whether he'd enjoyed his workout. He just stood there trying to catch his breath, and never bothered to answer me.

A few minutes later we discovered that what we had seen was not an airplane blowing up or any other airport incident, but the Henderson, Nevada rocket fuel plant exploding! When we learned further details, we found out that the blast had blown several cars off the freeway next to the plant, but no one, either in the plant or in the cars, had been injured. Amazingly, one man was actually inside the building when the explosion took place, but he happened to be standing behind a blast plate and wasn't hurt.

There's a reason I've been sharing all these old stories about my bands when the real topic of this part of my own journey is supposed to my struggles with alcohol. It's just my way of saying that a lot of situations in life can provide you with a 'get out of jail free' card for a while. You can often have a hell of a good time as you're slowly sinking further into your habit, but as you'll see when we get a little further into things, it's usually only a temporary reprieve.

During this whole time, I was drinking as much as ever and doing a bit more cocaine again, too, and I had Randy as a fully engaged partner in crime. Even though the other players were moderate in their habits, Randy and I were still going full tilt. And at the time, we had no idea how many other areas of our careers our behavior was affecting.

Hangin' Up the Spurs

Chapter Eleven

Not too long after we did our gig in Las Vegas, complete with a pyrotechnic encore, as well as a few more short trips to various places around the country, Randy came to me and said he had been offered a chance to rejoin Poco for a reunion album and tour. Capitol Records was allegedly willing to bonus the band a very healthy six-figure amount to put it together.

I really hated to see him go, but I told him he would be foolish to turn down that fat a payday. Our prospects were not bright enough to counterbalance such a rare opportunity. Besides, I had always liked the original Poco lineup.

The reunion they put together ultimately resulted in the 1989 album *Legacy*. As with many such endeavors, I think politics may have come into play—because what ended up happening with the *Legacy* project came nowhere near what had been promised. And in reality, I think the reason Randy left The Roberts-Meisner Band had as much to do with our lack of instant success as it had to do with Poco's offer.

He was also probably ready to take some time off. He was drinking and sniffing too much, and I was, too. Randy is one of the nicest, gentlest men I have ever had the pleasure of working with in this industry, as well as a truly great high tenor with a natural sense of harmony, but I believe he had never completely gotten over walking away from the Eagles. After all, he was an original member and they were well on their way to becoming one of the four or five most successful bands in rock history while he was still in the band. It was his decision to leave, but I think he felt he had been backed into a corner where he really had no other choice, if he wanted to maintain his self-respect.

After Randy left, we decided we should go ahead as a band, but we were going to have to change the name. Somehow the Roberts-? Band just didn't have the proper ring to it. I mulled over what I hoped the band might accomplish by putting some quality music out there in the air. That started a thought process chain in my mind. Sort of an equation for our future. If everything went right, it would be—good music equals popular acceptance equals fame equals financial gain. So if we were lucky, we'd end up rich and famous. Maybe that was the name for us. But I've always gone by Rick, and never Rich, so calling the band The Rich and Famous didn't make any sense. So instead, we decided to call ourselves The Rick and Famous.

The bassist we replaced Randy with was Gerald Johnson. Gerald had played with a whole lot of really good people, including The Steve Miller Band, The Sweet Inspirations, Stephen Stills, Dave Mason, The Pointer Sisters, Les Dudek, and numerous others. With his addition, we definitely didn't feel like we were giving anything away in quality. And though he couldn't duplicate Randy's voice, he was available to sing harmony parts.

With Cary and Bray and I, we still had three strong vocalists, and since Randy hadn't been writing much, we weren't losing a lot in the way of material. Of course, it was always nice to have some of his old Eagles hits in the show, like "Take It to the Limit" and "Try and Love Again", but our repertoire wasn't totally gutted.

Between the loss of Randy's name value and having to start all over establishing a reputation for the band, (because no one knew the new name) gigs got a little hard to find for a while. But we were confident things would pick up before long.

Another Trip to the Circus

My last 1980's commitment was something of a rewind. It was early in 1989 when I got a recall offer from *my* old band. Firefall had broken up when I left, but about a year later, Jock decided to put it back together with a new lineup. Since most of the best-known material, and nearly all the singles were my songs, when John Sambataro, who had been the lead singer since the reformation decided to quit, Jock called to ask me if I would be interested in rejoining the band. They were still performing all the hits and best known material from the old days so I wouldn't have to learn a whole new catalogue.

I really enjoyed the music The Rick and Famous were making, but I also really missed Colorado. Not to mention the lure of what Firefall had once been was very appealing. So once again, I thought maybe I could have my cake and eat it, too.

I accepted the offer, but since The Rick and Famous was still in existence, I embarked on nearly two and a half years of commuting between Boulder and L.A. Many times my commute was from L.A. to wherever Firefall was booked to play, but just as often my trip was to Colorado for rehearsal, photo sessions, or various other band-related business. And it didn't take long before I rediscovered my full tolerance and superior drinking ability on all those flights from LAX to wherever.

As time went by, my primary musical activity slowly but surely gravitated toward my dealings with Firefall, and away from The Rick and Famous. There just wasn't that much work out there for the RFB, and I couldn't afford to keep paying the band a weekly salary just to play the occasional engagement that came our way. Our chances for a record deal were looking pretty slim, so finally we decided to call it a day in early 1991. At that point, it was just a matter of time before I would abandon L.A. and go back to Colorado.

I can't say for sure whether rejoining Firefall was a good thing or a bad thing in terms of my drinking. It was a comfortable situation, being able to come back to a well-known band and sing the songs I knew so well. But I didn't feel as close to this version of the band as I had to my other groups. Maybe because all the guys now in the band had been playing together for at least two years when I was asked to come back. Comfortable, yes. But close, not so much.

The only remaining member from the original band was Jock Bartley, and he wasn't a drug or alcohol guy. Neither was anybody else in the band, so you might think it would be a healthy environment for me.

It was a curious situation. Here I was the new guy in a band that I had formed a decade and a half earlier. That felt kind of strange. I suppose I was especially sensitive to this since our shows still revolved heavily around my songs. It didn't help that I was still in Los Angeles while the rest of the guys lived in Colorado. It only added to the sense of emotional isolation I felt. But whatever the reasons, after I rejoined the band I didn't change my habits at all.

I did notice that the other members of the band were keeping an eye on me, but I wasn't sure whether they were clocking my alcohol intake, or just trying to figure out how much I intended to assert myself as an original member and former front man for the group. After a while and a few rather intense one-on-one conversations, it became clear that they had heard all the stories and wanted to be reassured that I was going to act like a grown-up.

By that time, I was doing a lot less cocaine, but I had minimized my drinking only enough to where I could do my work. Usually. The most convenient time for me to hit the bottle was out on the road, and after a couple of times when I overdid myself, the band was getting increasingly worried about whether they could count on me when we went out on stage.

I finally moved back to Colorado in August of 1991 thinking maybe I could get the situation back under control by returning to a place where I felt more at home. I'd get my feet back on the ground, and show the band they could depend on me. Boulder is a lot smaller than Los Angeles, with much less nightlife, and I hoped that a change of scene might motivate me to start living in the real world. Besides, since The Rick and Famous had broken up, there was no longer any reason to stick around Los Angeles. I asked the other guys in Firefall to keep their eyes open for a place I might rent, and the bass player managed to find one behind his own landlady's house.

Once the new place was all arranged, I packed up my things and said goodbye to California. This time I was driving my Toyota GTS, and it was the first time I'd ever driven the trip in that direction. With all those hours on the road, I found myself thinking over the recent past and taking stock of my situation. I realized I had just spent ten years in California, during which time I had discovered myself to be seriously in debt to the IRS, had a house foreclosed on, been through two bands and ten years without releasing any new music or otherwise moving forward in my career, increased the volume of my drinking, and just for toppers, been through the most devastating romantic relationship I had ever been involved in. All in all, I didn't count the '80s as one of the most shining or productive decades of my life.

And in addition to all that, I was just about to turn forty-two, so I was no longer operating with the same 'take a chance, and if it doesn't work out you can always start over' sensibility that I had had at twenty.

I even thought about the fact that I had made this same trip twice in the other direction, once in a BMW and once in a Mercedes, and now I was going back in a Toyota. I mean, my car was a great little set of wheels, but…you know what I'm saying. It was wonderful, but it wasn't any Mercedes. It was just one more reminder that things had changed greatly.

It was a study in reverse momentum. I was running backwards on the road to success. So there I was rolling down the highway with a Thermos of vodka and cranberry juice, and a couple of grams in my pocket. Suddenly for the first time, I really and truly came to grips with the fact that some changes needed to be made in almost *every* aspect of my life. I wasn't so much feeling sorry for myself. I was just analyzing the events and finding them unacceptable. I definitely needed to make some major adjustments if I expected the next ten years to be any better than the last ten.

* * *

For me, realizing something and implementing it were two separate things. The facts I was faced with didn't make enough of an impression on me at that point to make me willing to change my overall way of living, especially in terms of drugs and alcohol. I could see that my drinking had reached a point where it was affecting my performance level. Not every time, but more than once, and once is one time too many in my opinion. At least, that's how I feel about it now. Back then, I was able to isolate each occurrence in my mind and view it as an aberration instead of a steadily growing problem.

The only thing I did to even slightly alter my lifestyle was start to attend a few A.A. meetings. I believe A.A. is a wonderful organization, and has helped countless people who probably would never have managed to salvage their lives without it. But there are some people, of which I am one, for whom A.A. is not the answer. I can honestly say I never felt more like going out and downing a few than I did after almost every meeting I went to. Unfortunately, for me the meetings were depressing rather than inspiring.

But A.A. did one very important thing for me. Towards the end of 1991while at an A.A. meeting, I met the woman I had always dreamed of, in the flesh.

That happened to be Mary McKinney, my future wife. She was a startlingly beautiful woman, so when I saw her across the room at the meeting, I couldn't help noticing she looked a little out of place. A lot of the people in the room looked at the very least, sort of careworn, if not a bit bedraggled. She, on the other hand, appeared very composed and in control of herself. I didn't have the slightest idea then that she would eventually be the person who turned my life back around.

After the meeting was over, I caught up to her on the way out the door and told her how attractive I thought she was. That may sound a trifle forward to some, but it was normal behavior for me. I have made it a practice for as long as I can remember to tell a beautiful woman about my appreciation of that fact. Her answer totally disregarded my statement anyway.

She responded by saying, *"Aren't you Rick Roberts?"*

I told her I was, and asked her name. She told me who she was, and said we had met before. When I asked where, she explained, and slowly it all came back to me, including why I hadn't paid more attention to her the first time.

I asked her to lunch on the spot, and that was the beginning of a love affair that has still never ended.

It turns out I had been introduced to Mary about two years before at a Firefall show in Estes Park. At that time she was taking guitar lessons from Jock, and on that occasion he asked everyone in the band to keep their distance because she was his student and any hanky-panky might be awkward. It was fairly obvious that he was mainly speaking to me since I was the only romantically unencumbered member of the group. With all that going on, I had completely forgotten about ever meeting her.

And I found out why she appeared to be in so much better condition than most of the other people at A.A.; she had been completely sober for nearly seven years.

I learned later her full name was Mary Margaret McKinney. From that day forward, whenever I hear the old ballad, "My Wild Irish Rose", I can't help but think they might have had Ms. McKinney in mind.

* * *

Mary was a distinctly positive influence in my life so my time in Boulder got a little less crazy. I wasn't doing much drinking when she was around, and I spent

Lame Brain

the majority of my time between tour trips with her. I was of course drinking and sniffing when I was at home at night by myself, since that was the time I did my writing. Otherwise, I did most of my drinking when I was in hotel rooms on the road, or at the hotel bar after the shows. So, it was no wonder the other band members were concerned. I was trying to present the best side of myself to Mary, so conversely, those guys were left with the worst of me.

Things got a bit more complicated a few months later. Mary had moved back to Boulder primarily to take care of Henry Crossen, her mentor, and a man who had been like a second father to her. Henry had suffered a stroke and needed someone to look after him full-time. Mary had been living down in Nashville, but when she heard about his situation, she immediately came back to Colorado to help.

After she had been caring for him for a while, things developed in such a way that she needed to find a new place to live. His health was failing, and there were some other family tensions she needed to distance herself away from.

I asked Mary if she wanted to stay with me for a little while until she found herself a new place. And she agreed. Once she was in my house though, I didn't want her to leave. She felt the same way. We've been together ever since. The complication was that now I *was* going to have to rearrange my drinking habits.

Since she was a recovering alcoholic, I didn't want to drink around her. I also didn't want to give up my bottle. So I did what any thoughtful alcoholic would do. I formulated elaborate schemes and ruses to hide my boozing. I didn't try to claim I was alcohol-free, but I did try to downplay the extent of things.

I know she wasn't taken in, but having been down that road herself, she knew nothing she could say was going to alter my behavior. Mary made it clear that she didn't approve, but she also realized that the only person who could make the final choice for me to stop drinking was me.

The Elephant in the Room

Chapter Twelve

I made my second exit from Firefall in the spring of 1992. It was called "a mutual decision," but I think that if I had resisted the move, it wouldn't have been long before the group fired me anyway. The band was generous enough to let me walk away with my dignity intact. I didn't mind too much, because we were kind of treading water as far as our music was concerned. Not only were we doing exactly the same show featuring all the old hits for every performance, but the gigs were not as frequent as we would have liked. I was drinking more than ever and even *I* couldn't deny that I had developed a serious problem. Of course, I had started to "not deny that I had a serious problem" about ten years (and six chapters) back.

I guess I could claim there were a number of reasons, but none of them can legitimately excuse my behavior towards the end of my second stint with Firefall. The fact is, during my last few months with the band I was just coasting and had several shows where I really let my drinking get away from me. It still amazes me, even after all these years, how I could have let my professional pride gradually slip away to such a point and not even notice. Or if I *did* notice, then simply not to care enough to do anything about it.

A couple of chapters back, I mentioned that sometimes certain situations will provide you with a 'get out of jail free' card and a career in rock and roll is definitely one of those. It goes double if you happen to be supplying the musical material for your group. But I also made note of the fact that the reprieve was usually only temporary, and so it was for me. My performance level had slipped below an acceptable level, and writing new songs had become an increasingly rare occurrence. I had gone to the well a few too many times, and it had apparently run dry.

There are two shows that stand out in my memory as the very worst. One of them was at an outdoor gig at a place called Mishiwaka. It was a rural amphitheater on the Poudre River up near Ft. Collins, Colorado. We did one show in the afternoon and a second show in early evening. There were three or four hours between the sets, and with nothing else to do, I spent the whole time drinking. By the time we did the later show, I was trashed. Unfortunately, or maybe fortunately, someone filmed the show and I was strongly advised to watch it. When I did, I found it nothing less than humiliating.

But it didn't make me put down the bottle. All it did was provide me with a fleeting moment of regret.

The other instance was also at an outdoor, two-show gig. This time we were performing in Lexington, Kentucky. It was midsummer and not only very hot, but very humid. I was terribly hung over from the night before so I had a couple of "hair of the dog" drinks before we left the hotel for our first set. That got me through that one. But since we were out at a fairground, I didn't have an opportunity to recharge before the second show, and that's when things got ugly.

As I said, it was very hot and humid and about midway through the show I was getting thirsty. I had a big cup of cold water right at my feet, but when I reached down for it, I was shaking so bad I looked like I had some sort of palsy, so I decided to pass on even making the effort. I knew that even if I grabbed the cup, I would spill more of it than I would be able to get to my mouth. By that time, I was on a short leash with the band, and quite frankly, I was scared to further expose what kind of shape I was in by reaching for the water. I didn't want Firefall fans to see me in that condition, either. So, somehow I made it through the performance and then drank myself into a calmer frame of mind and body when I got back to the hotel. At least the shaking stopped.

I think that show may have been the one that sealed my fate. Even though I stayed in the band for a while longer after that, it was all over but the shouting. The only good thing about the situation was that since I was no longer benefitting by the use of cocaine, it was time to say goodbye to that drug once and for all. As I mentioned early on, kicking the habit presented no problem whatsoever. My reason for doing it was gone, so there was no longer any appeal to it.

The Days of Wine and Roses

Now that I was living with Mary, my time at home had become the highlight of my life. When I was there, I was keeping my drinking a little more under control and a lot more under wraps. The drinking I did do, I did primarily in the daytime hours, mostly in the latter part of the morning and the early afternoon while Mary was working. So if I cut myself off by midafternoon, I was usually in pretty good shape by the time she came home.

I always thought if I was going to drink with the intention of getting high, which I was then, it made more sense to do it when I could stay awake to enjoy the effects. I never saw the point in drinking in the evening when all you did was catch a buzz and then go to bed. Notice I say "getting high," not "getting trashed." Except for the one stretch of time at the end of a love affair gone wrong, I never drank with the intention of getting totally loaded. But I always appreciated that certain glow I got when I had a good buzz on. I hadn't found out yet that the glow eventually fades and doesn't come back.

Mary and I were falling more in love all the time. I know she saw my deeply entrenched alcoholism, but she stuck by me regardless. She had faith it would be only a matter of time until I woke up and got myself straightened out. I regret to say it took me a lot longer than she had figured on. I was still doing my best to hide the severity of my addiction. I guess I did at least a pretty good job of it, because when I asked her to be my wife, she said yes.

In the years since, more than one of my longtime friends has asked me how a guy like me managed to catch a woman like her. One possibility is that there really are such things as guardian angels, and she is mine. That's been suggested more than once. The only other thing I can think of is that this is one exception to the rule as far as what I think about being a nice drunk not necessarily being a good thing. Let me explain that.

Most people seem to think that if someone is going to be a drunk, one way or the other, it's not quite as terrible if the person is at least an inoffensive, quiet, and generally harmless drunk—what's known as a 'nice' or a 'polite' drunk.

I totally disagree.

Being that kind of a drunk may turn out to be the worst thing that could happen to an alcoholic. When you're a mean drunk and turn into a monster every time you have a few too many, your friends are going to let you know about it pretty quick. If you don't do something to clean up your act, before long you don't have any friends. But when you're the kind of drunk who doesn't ever make any trouble, who doesn't want to start a fight, or who maybe even gets a little funnier when you're high, you can get away with it for a long time. That's not the best thing. Some of your friends will look the other way and say things like *"Oh, that's just Ricky. He's harmless."* But what is being overlooked is that you're *not* harmless. You're harming *yourself* and those you love; and the ones who love you the most are usually the ones you hurt the most. The truly awful thing about addiction is how easy it makes it to fool *yourself*.

I should also make it clear that no matter what it sounds like from my narrative, I was *not* drunk all the time. But I did drink on an almost daily basis, some days more than others. But I was okay, because "I was a nice drunk." I get it.

* * *

Lame Brain

Mary and I tied the knot on May 23rd, 1993 at a house in the mountains of Colorado. My old friends, Henry and Susie, were the best man and the matron of honor. It was their house, and they thought a lot more of Mary than they had of Loretta. In fact, they were crazy about my wife-to-be and felt like I had won the lady lottery. They thought I was getting a much better deal by linking my future to a sane woman rather than…well, you know. I was forty-three and Mary was thirty. It was the first time down the aisle for both of us because we had the same concept concerning matrimony. We believed marriage was something you try your best to do only once, and when you do, you had better honor the vows!

I don't mean to sound preachy, but I had seen too many of my friends and peers in music take marriage too casually, as if it was no more of a commitment than going steady in high school. If you got bored or hit a rough spot, you just broke up. And that's especially true for those in the rarified atmosphere of being a successful musician where there were usually a dozen other willing young women waiting for their chance to give it a try with you. As such, it's easy to start believing there will always be someone just as good, if not even better, waiting around the corner. Life in the rock and roll world can lead to a lot of unrealistic perceptions about things, but this is one of the cruelest.

When you're out there in some variety of the spotlight every waking hour it can distort your sense of reality. A lot of people cater to your every wish and treat you as if you are a unique and extraordinary individual. They make you feel like you can do no wrong.

And take it from me, you don't have to be too much of a star for the syndrome to kick in. It's amazing how completely some people buy into it, both the performers and the fans. By the time everyone gets an accurate read on things, a lot of damage can have already occurred. And that includes some badly broken hearts.

Mary and I didn't want to join that club, and as I write this, we've just celebrated our twenty-second anniversary with twenty-four years together. I'm not saying there haven't been some trying times, but nobody gets to slide through without a few bruises. More than a few of our bruises came as a result of my drinking, but through it all, Mary stood by me.

Even after we married, my journey back to sobriety was still going to be a long and circuitous one and it hadn't even started yet. I would get quite a way deeper down before I started to climb out of the hole I was still digging.

One of the things that take longest for most alcoholics to realize and accept is the collateral damage caused by their alcoholism. I was no exception. I was so wrapped up in my own liquor-altered reality that it totally escaped my attention that I was now expected to share my life with another human being—someone I loved. I've always tried to support and encourage Mary in all her endeavors, but in those days, I was a whole lot less than a full-time partner. It wasn't because I didn't want to be. It just never occurred to me that my attention was not reaching very far beyond my own needs and desires.

Maybe one of the most unattractive aspects in the personality of an alcoholic is the overwhelming selfishness it breeds in those afflicted. That's not a secret. But, one of the saddest things is our own inability to recognize that fact.

As for me, I wandered around in a self-inflicted haze for years before I got it through my thick head that everything in my life wasn't all about me.

* * *

I've gotten a little caught up in talking about my marriage, but that's the area of my life that was most impacted by my drinking. I had all but left my music career behind me, and I still hadn't figured out *how* that had happened. More accurately, I refused to *face* the reason why it had happened.

The next few years were among the most uneven of my adult life, and can be summed up in a few short sentences.

About the time I was married, I got aboard a roller coaster, going up and down very quickly. Not that I necessarily wanted to get off, but I was taken by surprise by the twists and turns. The marriage was responsible for most of the ups and the liquor caused most of the downs.

So that's *what* made things so uneven. Explaining *why* things were uneven will take a little longer.

On the upside, I had married a wonderful woman who made my life more complete in almost every way. Being married involved a great number of changes in my way of thinking, because as I said, both Mary and I took our commitment very seriously. Even though I had lived with several women in the past, and was not only in love with them, but hoping to build something permanent, there was always the knowledge we had not made a lifetime choice. The whole reason for holding off on marriage was to get to know each other well enough to be willing to take the last, most binding step. Without committing myself to marriage vows, I always knew that if a relationship didn't stand up to any test fate or circumstance might throw at us, I could walk away. But that ability to carelessly end a relationship was something I made up my mind to put aside when I said 'I do.' That's what I mean about some people looking at marriage too casually. I figure that if you carry that escape clause, the awareness that you can always walk away if things start to get *too* tough attitude into your marriage, then you've jumped the gun.

Anyway, the changes in my thinking were focused on the facts of real life as a team, and all the responsibilities that were no longer just an option. That, and the realization a good marriage depends in part on learning how to compromise in a way that leaves both of you satisfied. The marriage stands a much smaller chance of working if one of you insists on everything being your way. Even if

Lame Brain

the arrangement survives, when it only serves the needs or the will of one of the partners, it's a marriage in name only. The other so called 'partner' becomes more of an indentured servant.

I had every intention of trying my best to be a part of our team. Until it came to giving up the bottle. I was unwilling to accept the fact that my alcohol use (and clinging to it) was part of the deal, too.

But we're still talking about the way it should be—the upside. There was also a definite downside happening, and it involved primarily what was going on with my drinking. Drinking was part of the cause of my dissatisfaction, and also partly a result of the same thing. But the real underlying cause of my discontentment was that I missed my musical career—the whole shebang—playing, performing, creating, etcetera.

I had not given up my music for the sake of getting married, nor was my marriage the reason my career had gone into eclipse. But without any active participation in music, the boredom factor had begun to loom ever larger. And boredom is just something I've never done very well with at all. When I say those years were uneven, I think it was due in great measure to not knowing what to do with myself and therefore having way too much time on my hands. I call it boredom, but it was really inertia created by uncertainty. Even before Mary and I got married, starting shortly after Firefall and I had parted company, I was beginning to feel restless about not doing anything with my music. In fact, that feeling of stagnation may have started to take root while I was still in my second stint with the band, because it felt like that wasn't going anywhere either. I made light of it to my friends, saying I was semi-retired and enjoying a little well-earned rest. That wasn't really what was going on, though.

In truth, I was confused about what my options were. As a result, I was making false starts in several directions without any sort of game plan. I didn't even have the common sense or the clarity of mind to realize I wouldn't be able to get things together without the help of some people who were a great deal more knowledgeable in the area of musical career planning.

I tried to book myself into a few solo gigs, but I wasn't very organized about it, nor did it cause much excitement. I billed the concert dates as *"An Evening with the Composer"*, because I planned on doing a lot of my songs that people were familiar with hearing, but who had only heard the arrangements that were on the Burrito Brothers' and Firefall's records. I didn't want the audience coming in expecting all the bells and whistles of the recorded versions. I wanted to let them know in advance that what they were going to hear were the songs just the way they sounded at three o'clock in the morning in my living room when I wrote them. But I don't know if all that many people understood the message I was trying to deliver.

By this time, in my heart of hearts, I knew I was better off playing with a band, but I also knew from experience just how much time, commitment, dedication, compatibility, and flat-out hard work it took to put a band together.

Since I was already back with Firefall when I returned to Boulder, I wasn't out and about in the community the way I had been before I left. By the time I left the band, Mary and I were living together, so I still wasn't going out that much. Add the fact I was now in my forties and not particularly interested in making the club scene anyway.

The result was that it took me a while to realize just how much Boulder had changed in the last decade. So even if I had wanted to put together a new band, I'm not sure I would have known where to start.

Instead, I sat at home and tried to formulate some other way to build some momentum toward restarting my career and getting nowhere fast. Naturally, I was trying to "help" my brainstorming process with a large amount of alcohol.

Meanwhile, even though my governmental indemnity had long since become just another piece in the background music of my life, a personal visit one day from an IRS agent brought my tax situation fully back to my attention. That wake-up call, combined with becoming a husband, gave me the feeling I was getting a bit out of my depth. There was suddenly much more going on than I was prepared (or able) to deal with, and I didn't know where to turn for advice.

One thing that had me confused was discovering the many new dimensions of my life as part of a team. It was very interesting, to say the least. I was alerted to a world of previously undreamed of responsibilities, and one of the primary things was to be a provider. Since all my money coming in was from royalties, I didn't feel I was living up to my financial obligations. My royalties represented something I had already done, and I felt I should be producing something more current. That was doubly true because of all the outstanding financial burdens that kept us in a position of, just like the old days, 'getting by,' but not getting ahead. And through it all, I was still unable or unwilling to recognize my drinking as one of, if not the main source of, our problems.

Somewhere in there I got my first DUI. I know it's hard to believe I could have slipped through without ever facing any repercussions stemming from my behavior for so many years, but that's how it had all gone down. And because of the lack of consequences, I had never had to consider the cause and effect aspect of my actions. Every minor brush I had had with the authorities until that time was muddied up with some additional factor. I could always find some explanation that allowed me to see the experience as happening due to something other than my drinking.

With that sense of denial (which is what it was), I had been able to fool myself into thinking that at least I was keeping that part of my relationship with alcohol under some control. Even though I had long since accepted the fact I had a major league alcohol problem, it somehow wasn't getting through to me that my problem was anything more than just consuming too much booze. That's all I saw. I still wasn't extrapolating on all the effects my drinking had on the people in my life. As far as I was concerned, even the end of my relationship with Firefall seemed to be more attributable to the band's lack of progress than to my own actions. I felt all of what had happened was because my heart wasn't in it, not at all because of my drinking habits.

I was totally blind to the ripple effect of how my actions impacted everything and everybody around me, and that the problems were all created by me and my bottle. In other words, I was in a *classic* state of denial. When I got the DUI, everything suddenly took on a whole new reality.

Maybe a pretty good yardstick of how deeply I was into my addiction is the fact, even now, I'm still a little unclear on a lot of the details of how things unfolded that day. And I'm not talking about a blackout or anything like that. Just an overall blurry sense about the sequence of events, as well as that whole period of my life. I vaguely remember how the whole deal came down. Considering the importance of that episode to my future perspective on drinking, it's hard to believe every detail is not etched indelibly into my memory. After all, it *was* a major event. From then almost until I finally put down the habit once and for all, I would be tangled up with the law and the authorities one way or another.

But here's what I can remember about that day. I was driving down to Denver late one morning and I had already had several drinks. I realized my tolerance had deserted me that day, so I got off at one of the exits and drove into a suburban neighborhood. Then, I pulled over to the side of the road to take a nap.

The next thing I knew there was a police officer knocking on my car window. I rolled it down, and he asked me what I was doing there. When I answered, it was obvious from the way he jerked back that he could smell the strong aroma of alcohol on my breath. He put me through the roadside sobriety test. I didn't pass. It was still the middle part of the '90s (1995, I think), and local law enforcement hadn't gotten quite as stringent about alcohol-related, non-accident situations as they would soon become. Nonetheless, I got hauled down to the station, was cited for public drunkenness, issued a DUI, and had to have Mary bus it down to pick me up and take me home. Fortunately, since the car wasn't in motion and the engine wasn't operating, the authorities chose to go easy on me and not take things any further. But it *was* still my first DUI, and there would be a mandatory court appearance.

Now that my drinking was becoming a danger to others besides myself, as well as to our private lives, Mary couldn't let it slip by anymore. She told me it was obvious I needed help, and maybe it was time for me to go into a rehab program. I, of course, was somewhat less than enthused by the idea, but she made it clear it was not up to me alone. The courts were going to have some say in the matter, too. When I finally took an honest look at things, I knew she was right on all counts.

We researched a few programs and chose one outside of Colorado Springs called The Ark at Green Mountain Falls. It was a thirty-day program, and would be the first of about seven or eight rehabs I went into over the next ten years. In the end, all of them were good and should have given me enough motivation to change my ways, but they didn't. I was too stupid and stubborn to see that I was slowly but steadily killing myself.

What finally convinced me to stop once and for all was an accidental encounter with the wrong medication, the continuing support and strength of Mary, and of course, boredom. That combination of unrelated elements may not make much sense now, but you'll see what I mean...

In a Galaxy Far, Far, Away

Chapter Thirteen

I can honestly say that I wasn't trying to pull a fast one on the legal system by my proactive enrollment at Green Mountain. I thought it might be a chance to change course and start a new chapter in my life. I could see that things were getting way beyond my ability to control again, and now that I had crossed the line between harming myself and potentially harming others, it was plainly time to up the ante. Rehab seemed like the logical next step. Now, I'm aware of how many times I've talked about coming to the conclusion that things were getting out of control, or realizing I had a serious problem, or all the other ways I've said the same thing. There's a reason for that. I *was* looking to make a change. Every time. And every time I came to that realization, I thought I really meant it. You'll be reading about my *sudden awakening* several more times before the end of this book. Sometimes it takes a while before a person finally gets the message. The only thing I can say in my defense for taking so long to come around in making a change is by sharing a line from a song I wrote.

A hundred times you bleed
For once that you succeed
*But once is all you need**

Now, back to my story…

Since I was able to make the legitimate claim to the court that I was voluntarily entering a rehab program, they went easy on me. My driver's license was suspended for six months, but beyond that, all I was required to do was present documentation that I had successfully completed the program. The judge gave me three months to do it.

*From "Once Is All You Need", copyright © 1982 by Warner Tamerlane/El Sueno Music, BMI.

So off I went to Green Mountain. For the most part, I breezed right through it. I learned quite a bit about the short and long-term effects of drinking on the mind and the body. I was also reminded of a great deal I already knew, and that certainly didn't hurt either. The staff at the Ark was very knowledgeable and quite compassionate to the different circumstances of each client, and they kept things interesting with enough diversions to soften the feeling of confinement that comes with rehab.

Although not too far from Colorado Springs, the facility was actually outside of the city. It was composed of a mixed indoor-outdoor campus so the atmosphere of the place was very peaceful and pleasant. The staff took us for nature walks in the surrounding area and we were always free to roam around the grounds. There was even one day when they took us to a nearby horse ranch and we all had the opportunity to ride up the mountain trails on horseback. Mary came down a couple of times and brought home-baked treats for me and everyone else, too. In some ways, it was like a healthy summer vacation.

They also operated on the assumption that we all had a real desire to change our behavior. That was where they made their mistake with me. Not so much in the short-term, because I was really there with a very sincere desire to kick my habit. No, their mistake was in thinking I understood what my real demons were.

Even though I entered treatment with the best of intentions, the truth of the matter was that I wasn't prepared to stop drinking. I don't mean I wasn't ready, as in 'I don't want to stop yet.' I hadn't really discovered yet what motivated me to drink, so I didn't have the tools to permanently change the equation. Until you can accurately isolate the problem, you won't find a workable solution. Therefore, I wasn't prepared.

And the tricky part was I didn't even realize it. I did my best to implement every suggestion they offered to modify my attitudes. I wasn't trying to pull off some kind of con job to make anyone think I had seen the error of my ways and was on my way to a whole new lifestyle. It was no con job. I didn't spend my time there devising devious plots to fool them, and I wasn't counting the days until graduation with the foregone conclusion that I would pick up where I left off. But I did count the days, because I was anxious to get back to my wife and home.

The counselors and instructors there put some very good information at my disposal, coupled with some strategies that would help me *not to fall back* into old habits. But the one thing they had no way to prepare me for, or to counteract, was the excess of time I had on my hands when I got home. Most of the other people I went through the program with were going back to jobs and the responsibility of making a living. As I said before, Mary and I were not exactly getting ahead financially, but we were getting along. You might say we were doing just well enough to delude me into thinking everything could go on

Lame Brain

the way it was for as long as I wanted. I wasn't under the gun to go out and find a job to pay the rent or put food on the table. My royalties were enough to cover that, plus my ongoing IRS encumbrance.

Actually, going in search of work was not really a very promising option. I had spent my entire adult life in music, and so I found myself in my mid-forties totally lacking in any marketable job skills. In most professions that someone has spent a long time doing, it's hard not to pick a certain amount of peripheral knowledge that will help pave the way into a related line of work. I considered the potential areas of employment that might be open to me. But I soon discovered that most of them were either dependent on the technical expertise that was never my strong suit (sound man, engineer) or else required a broader familiarity with the nuts and bolts of music education than I had. To teach voice or even give singing lessons you need to be able to read music. That was a skill I had learned in high school and unlearned in thirty-five years of rock and roll. And it meant going back to school. School could be very expensive—and not very appealing. So, I was stuck.

* * *

My personal opinion is that thirty days is not necessarily enough time to clear the mind of anyone with an alcohol habit, and certainly not someone who had been drinking as *long* and as *much* as I had. And considering that I hadn't personally plumbed the deepest depths of what drinking could do, there wasn't the sense of urgency or a life or death choice hanging over me. I'd never been through the DT's, or awakened to find I had totally lost any recollection of the previous two or three days. I guess I'm lucky that I never did have to experience those horrors. The most earthshaking experience I'd had was the DUI, and in *my* mind, even that was a fairly harmless one. There had been no accident, and no one hurt. The only real inconvenience to me that resulted from it all was having my driver's license suspended for a while. I realize now that my perceptions were way off the mark, but that's what I mean about thirty days not being enough to clear a person's head.

So ultimately, when I went back home, I was able to stay away from the booze for a while. But it wasn't long before the tedium of my day-to-day life became unbearable and I found myself drinking again. For a certain span of time, I was drinking somewhat less, although with my tolerance acquired through years of earnest practice, I was soon downing larger and larger amounts. Of course the old hide-and-seek game was back in play, not only as far as when I drank, but also in the actual hiding of my bottle. As far as Mary was concerned, I was supposed to be completely clean, so I was using my best creative talents to find truly remarkable places to stash my liquor. I won't reveal any of those, because I don't want to inspire any other would-be stashers. Suffice it to say that getting to some of my hiding places provided me with more actual physical exercise than any other single activity in my life at that time.

Before long, it became clear that Mary at least suspected I was hitting the bottle again, but I was devious enough to prevent her from finding any concrete evidence to confront me. So, she was put in a position of biding her time until she could get into a better situation to address the issue. She showed remarkable patience in waiting me out.

Just like at so many other points in my life, my drinking was part of another self-perpetuating situation. I drank because I was bored; I was bored because I wasn't doing anything; I wasn't doing anything because my desire to do anything was dulled by my drinking. Round and round we go. I keep referring to the self-perpetuating aspects of my drinking. I think it is called circular reasoning. Crazy people do it.

I tried to cover up my lack of activity by attempting to write songs, but my songwriting was suffering from a lack of interest or inspiration, too. And the whole time I was going right along each day with the same happy-go-lucky attitude that I always had.

It sounds strange, but at that point in my life I *was* happy. As I have mentioned, I have a wonderful wife, and back then, in most ways life was good. I couldn't shake the underlying feeling that I was spinning my wheels, but there were always a lot of things to keep me smiling. I've been a hopeless optimist all my life, so it has never taken much to keep my spirits up. I spent my days reading, watching TV, and playing a little music when the spirit moved me, but I had no desire to actually *do* anything. Mostly, I was just watching the world go by.

That feeling of spinning my wheels didn't exactly go away, and instead it rapidly became the norm. I drifted through the months without paying too much attention to the harsh reality that my life was in a total holding pattern. As I look back at it now, I can see that this was a new, lower level in the downward spiral my life was taking. I didn't even recognize the overwhelming sense of apathy that had taken hold in my mind. And that's coming from the running start on how uninvolved I had been before that. With the exception of Mary, I just didn't care about anything. Even my interest in music was becoming very peripheral—just hit and miss.

I was sublimating a lot of things by concentrating my attention on my home life, and with that as a focal point, I was able to ignore that I was accomplishing absolutely nothing elsewhere.

I'm being fairly generous to myself when I say I concentrated on my home life. If I'd really been the slightest bit honest with myself, I would have had to face the fact that I was contributing very little there, either. Since I wasn't working and I couldn't drive anywhere, I hung around the house at loose ends, with no obligations or responsibilities. I was living my life with no discipline whatsoever. Aside from my clandestine liquor runs, the only time I went out (on the bus) was to do errands like grocery shopping or going to the post office, and I only did those things when I felt like it.

Occasionally I mowed the lawn or did a bit of yard work, but nothing too complicated or demanding. I was writing a little, but as I said, I didn't have a lot of creative drive.

Mary managed to get me to join a gym with her, and we worked out regularly. While she was spending an hour on her routine, I would exercise for about half that time and then clean up so I could slip out to grab a couple of quick drinks at the nearest bar. There was no way to hide the fact that I was leaving the gym, so I devised a clever plan. Every time I left the gym early, I stopped off at a wonderful store called Art Mart that was nearby. They carried an incredibly diverse collection of bric-a-brac and art items, all of which were top quality. From among said items I would purchase a gift for Mary. I bought her Indian stone fetishes, beautifully carved mahogany animals and various other pieces. When I tallied my accounts, I found that my couple of morning drinks were costing me an average of thirty dollars a pop.

Naturally, I eventually wound up facing the prospect of another rehab program because even Mary's incredible patience was wearing thin.

One day we got into the car to allegedly run some innocuous errands. The next thing I knew we were at the Harmony Foundation in Estes Park. Harmony is a nationally known and highly successful treatment program, and Mary had a number of friends among the instructors up there that she thought might be able to get it through my thick skull exactly what I was doing to myself.

Mary is a recovering alcoholic, too, but the difference between us was that she came to her senses long before I ever met her. It only took one treatment program for her to get her head on straight, and she had already been sober for nearly seven years when we got together. That's one reason she was able to be so patient. She had been down the same road herself. She was simply hoping the folks at Harmony might open *my* eyes.

That day, I was somehow able to convince her that the trip up there, and facing the reality of being forced into treatment not by the legal system, but by someone I loved, had awakened me to the severity of the problem. If she would give me one more chance, I would get myself together. By doing that, I succeeded in postponing my entry into Harmony by about three months. *Because it was all a charade.* My promise was a bluff—nothing changed, and I had just managed to put things off for a little while.

In hindsight, I can see that some of the great lengths I was going to were only to help me avoid facing one hard fact. I couldn't seem to get it through my head that the pattern I had chosen to take on was in no way a game or a party. It was a sure fire way to an early grave. The party was over. Even my periodic sudden realizations about my drinking problem and how I had to clean up my act weren't an acceptance of the fact that my behavior could actually kill me.

I had let my experiences in the music world desensitize me more than I was aware. But deep down I think I did know the real truth, and I was doing all I could to keep that nasty piece of information from surfacing. I was playing a very dangerous version of 'ignorance is bliss.'

I have a good friend who went through the same era in music that I did, and he calls the '70s the "decade of death." So many of my peers and personal friends in music died at young ages for totally unnecessary reasons, all involving substance abuse and alcohol addiction, that I had grown callous to self-inflicted danger; death had lost its shock value and its impact. I had more or less ceased to consider cause and effect between my actions and their consequences and the same scenario as it related to others. To put it another way, I just figured *"It could never happen to me."*

Earlier, I lamented the loss of some of my old friends who are no longer with us. Probably the best example of my lack of attention was the death of Michael Clarke. He was one of my best friends and band mates from the day I got into the major leagues of music, and he had died as a direct result of alcoholism only two years before the first time I set foot in rehab. That should have been as clear a message as anyone could send me. The damage to his body and the pain he endured before he finally expired was too nightmarish to believe. He even spoke out publicly about how much he regretted the choices he had made and urged others not to make the same mistakes. But I wasn't listening.

Gene Clark was another guy I played together with, and even shared rooms with during the Byrds Salute band. He passed away six months prior to Michael for almost the exact same reasons. His death was also a warning I chose to ignore. And with Gene, the evidence was even plainer about how completely the addiction took control of his life. Less than a year before his death, he had had a third of his stomach surgically removed as a result of how he had treated his body.

At that point he was advised by his doctors that if he continued to drink and drug, then for all intents and purposes his fate was sealed. There would be nothing anyone could do to save him. Gene never even broke stride or slow downed. In eight months he was dead. But I was oblivious to it all. I just wasn't seeing the obvious parallel between their behavior and my own.

I did eventually end up at Harmony anyway, and did a thirty-day stint there, marking my second trip to rehab. The rules were a lot stricter at Harmony than at Green Mountain. Even though the facility was located in the mountains and was somewhat isolated from anything tempting, we were not allowed outside the main building except to go to and from our cabins in the morning and at bedtime.

The staff there was world class, and had enjoyed a high success rate with the people who went through the program.

Once again, I went voluntarily and with the best of intentions, and once again

Lame Brain

the ultimate results were the same. I was on the wagon for a couple of months after I graduated and then slowly slipped right back into my old patterns. The only difference that time was that the staff at Harmony put a lot of stock into nutritional considerations, so when I returned home, I followed a very healthy diet. Between that, and the fact that I have never smoked cigarettes, I figured I was taking pretty good care of myself. The classic happy idiot.

I can't name the exact date, but sometime in that general time period I got my next DUI. It was around eleven in the morning and I had consumed my usual couple of morning drinks. This time I didn't feel drunk, nor was I driving recklessly or like a drunk. But I was speeding through a school zone, doing about 35 mph in a 20 mph area. Classes were in session so there were no kids around, but the slower limits were still in effect. The officer smelled liquor on my breath, and took me in. I had only had my license back for a month or two.

To make a long story short, after the court appearance and the other associated legalities of an alcohol-related charge, they put me on probation for six months and suspended my license again—this time for a full year. The court ruling also required me to do daily breath analysis checks for that same probationary six months' time. That was not even a nuisance as far as drinking was concerned. There was a designated testing place within walking distance of my home, so I would amble over there in the late morning and get my blood alcohol level test done. I would also take along about four of those little miniature bottles of vodka and drink them on the way back to my house.

At home, I already had an established routine. Mary would leave for work soon after my return, and I would dig out my hidden bottle and have three or four more drinks. I had a measuring cup and knew exactly how much alcohol I could consume and still be clean by the time of my next breathalyzer. I also made sure that even though there might be booze in my system, I was sober in my actions by the time Mary came home.

I'm sure I wasn't fooling her completely, if at all, but she gave me the benefit of the doubt. She knew I was going to have to actually *want* to stop before anything would ever change.

A very scary concept had taken root in my mind by then. A large part of me had more or less subconsciously accepted the fact that I wasn't ever going to completely stop drinking. It wasn't a conscious decision or acceptance, but I can see from my perspective now that a truce (not quite a surrender) had been struck within me.

My conscious outlook was that I would quit sometime, just not quite yet. So at that point, I wasn't so much trying to quit as to stay within the boundaries and not get in any more trouble. And even that attitude lacked consistency.

It was cyclic. By the time I eventually started each new rehab, I would have managed to convince myself again that it would be different and *this time* I would stay sober after I finished the program. But it never changed. The problem was that I still didn't grasp the ultimate outcome of things. My addiction had totally blotted out my old memories of watching my mother finally become aware that she was about to lose her family to her habit. It was yet another case of failing to use what I had seen happen to others and apply it to myself.

The Circle Tightens

Another way to describe the period of time from the mid '90s to the middle of 2004 is as a decade of putting off the inevitable. In the last chapter I talked about it being a very uneven period, and in many ways, both those statements address the same issue. During those years, I spent far too much time bouncing around between periods of sobriety and going off the wagon with the same type of destination in store. Even though some of the details might change, eventually and inevitably, there was always another rehab program I entered with good intentions and an imagined sense of resolve that at last I was going to make the final break from alcohol. To put it in short form, I wasted about ten years.

I went through Parker Valley Hope twice with Westpines Lutheran in between, and two others I don't even remember the names of scattered in there. Since I always *thought* I was ready to make a change, I generally did well as I went through each program.

There was one exception. The court decided I had to do another stint in rehab after I miscalculated my measured daily intake and blew hot on a breath test. The center was in Greeley, Colorado, and was different from the rest. The program itself was state run and really not up to the standards of the ones I had been through before. Although I'm sure the staff there was doing their best with the resources they had, the clients were *all* court-ordered intakes and not the sort of people who were volunteering to straighten out their lives.

Most of the classes were nothing more than group therapy with about a dozen other addicted people who were more interested in cutting each other to pieces than trying to build one another's confidence or work towards getting healthy again. They were basically just finger-pointing sessions focused on the "I'm not as bad as you" syndrome. The program there also allowed every person in residence to have three hours of liberty on their own in town every day. Which was probably not the best idea for that particular clientele.

I have to say that particular program didn't work out too well for me. I went out one day on my free time after a particularly disgusting group therapy session, which had left one young woman in hysterical tears and two of the guys in a fistfight. Without even thinking of the consequences, I went into a local liquor store and bought a half-pint bottle of vodka and drank most of it. When

Lame Brain

I came back to the facility after my liberty time, one of my peers smelled it on my breath and reported me. So I got booted.

By this time the court had started to lose patience with me. They had mandated my trip to Greeley, but when I was dismissed from there I was sentenced to six months at Camp George West in Golden, Colorado.

That trip started with a four-week stay at the Boulder County Jail, and during that time something took place which is the only thing I can't forgive the system for.

I know I'm the one responsible for being where I was, but while I languished at the county slam my mother passed away. That was in October of 1997. I don't know the exact date, because when she died she was living alone, and they discovered her body a day or two later. I requested a temporary release to go to Florida and attend her funeral, but I was denied as being a *flight risk* and a danger to the community. I've been told my probation officer put the kibosh on my going and I have never quite understood that.

I had never been in trouble for anything other than alcohol or drugs. Even when the judge sentenced me, I was home for a few days before having to appear at the jail and surrender myself. I did that, and I don't see what caused the probation officer to think I was going to take a chance on going on the lam. But for some reason, she did. So I sat in jail and never got to say goodbye to my mom. I think any one of us needs closure in their lives for an event as significant as the loss of their mother. I was denied that and it left me with a tiny hole in my soul I won't ever be able to fill.

Consequently, that four weeks at "county" seemed to last forever, even though I knew it was probably going to be the briefest portion of my upcoming journey. Every day dragged by while memories of my mother dominated my thoughts. My surroundings were a constant reminder of the trip to Florida I hadn't gotten to take. I prayed that the authorities would finish the paperwork or whatever it was taking so long and get me out of there to the place where I would serve my sentence. I started to think maybe my case had fallen through the cracks and they'd lost track of me. But they hadn't forgotten me. They were just very slow. Eventually, they completed my transfer to Camp George West, and *then* forgot about me.

Camp Winnebago

Chapter Fourteen

Camp George West was a minimum-security detention center, and a lot more like a work camp than a jail. We weren't even forced to work that much. There were no bars or even doors on our rooms and nothing but a chain link fence around the property. It had a parking lot style bar that could be raised across the entrance when people were coming or going. We were able to move freely around the camp, and once we had finished our assigned chores, our time was our own.

Regulations had been even looser up until a few months before I got there. The inmates were allowed the privilege of going up to the corner convenience store to buy odds and ends like candy, cookies, chips, or other snacks. Unfortunately, a couple of inmates who didn't appreciate the fact they had a good thing started shoplifting and that privilege was soon taken away.

They allowed us to play board games and card games, and although no gambling was allowed, I'm pretty sure there was some subtle system in place that managed to make betting possible. Almost everyone had a TV in his room, but no cable. I wasn't too surprised to learn that the favorite shows in the camp were The Jerry Springer Show and any NASCAR racing event. Hockey was also a big winner, although a lot of the viewers tended to cheer for both teams—as long as there was a lot of fighting. I suspect quite a few of those watching didn't know all that much about the sport.

I ended up serving about three months there and becoming a minor celebrity due to my musical accomplishments. Maybe celebrity isn't the right way to say it. Let's just say that the word was out that I had been a "known person" with a public profile at one time, and a number of the other residents had a lot of questions about what it was like to be in the spotlight—even if they didn't know *what spotlight*. But despite its moderately casual regimen, since it was the only time I had ever been incarcerated, it was an incredibly long three months. In my mind, I felt like I was in Alcatraz. It's too bad they didn't allow me to have a guitar there, because I could really have written some funky blues tunes during my stay. Move over Johnny Cash!

I did make some very unusual friends and acquaintances while I was there, though.

The first person I came into contact with had been a guest of the corrections system for about twenty-five years, and had been at George West for nearly five. After all these years, and since I don't particularly cherish those memories, I'm ashamed to say I couldn't remember his name until Mary reminded me. His name was Reese.

She'd met Reese the first time she came to visit me. I can still picture him clearly. He was a white man of medium height and weight, with brown hair and brown eyes. He wouldn't have particularly stood out in any crowd. But when he told me his story, it left a very distinct impression on me.

When he was eighteen, Reese lived in one of the small farming towns of eastern Colorado. One night he got drunk and went out with only one purpose in mind. He told me he had decided that somebody was going to die that night. Before the night was over, he shot and killed a man in a convenience store outside of town. Nobody had attacked or provoked him into committing his crime. He was soon arrested and accused of first-degree murder. The one thing he never told me was whether he pleaded guilty or not guilty. It hardly matters, though. It was an open and shut case anyway.

He was convicted and sentenced to life imprisonment. The court originally sent him to a maximum-security prison, but before long it was clear that he not only regretted his crime, but intended to mold himself into a better person.

At the point when I met him, he had worked his way through the system from maximum security to minimum at George West. He had taught himself to play guitar. By reading and doing in-house testing (computers hadn't yet swept the country and there were no available online universities to the prison), I think he had accumulated enough credits to get his bachelor's degree, and he was now the camp librarian.

Since he was still a reader and so was I, we had several conversations before he told me his story. When he found out about my musical past and saw how clueless I was about proper jail behavior, he kind of took me under his wing. He showed me how to not get my ass kicked or even possibly wind up dead. All he asked in return was that I give him a few pointers on the guitar. He was the only guy in the whole camp who was allowed to have an instrument.

I know it might sound hard to believe, but from what I could see he had become an extremely gentle person. It was hard for *me* to believe he had done what he had. He was also one of the most intelligent and thoughtful men I came across at the camp. He had accepted all responsibility for his terrible crime, and made no excuses or rationalizations for why it had happened. He was pretty certain he would never be granted parole so he had adjusted to the life he had determined for himself, and made up his mind to make the best of it.

On the other end of the spectrum, it was while I was there that I found a reason to be truly physically afraid for the first time since I was a kid. There was a Latino guy that I never actually met, but who had for some reason chosen me as the target for his abundant hatred. Every time we crossed paths within the small confines of the camp, he gave me a look of such incredible venom that I was frightened he would attack me on the spot. He wasn't all that much bigger than I was, but he had the look of a no-holds-barred street fighter. I've never claimed to be a bad ass, and I was pretty sure he could do me some serious damage if he tried. But I have to say, he wasn't very representative of the general population in there.

Most of the inmates fell somewhere in the middle. They were neither hardened criminals nor solid, law-abiding citizens. With the exception of a few who, like Reese, had worked their way through the system after committing some serious crime, the majority were in for first offenses or mid-level non-violent crimes.

I was struck by the fact that quite a lot of the men in there seemed to be at least mildly eccentric. I couldn't help wondering whether their quirks were for real or some kind of low-level defense mechanism. If you seem slightly loony, people tend to let you have your space and don't take it too personally if you say something offensive. One case in point I remember was a very quiet man who had caught a mouse and tamed it to be his pet. He must have fed it and slowly trained it, because it would sit on his hand or ride in the pocket of his coat. I can't remember the guy's name but the mouse's name was Bruiser.

There weren't too many organized events or classes at the camp. The only scheduled activity I took part in was the in-house concert choir. I won't say too much about that, except we weren't in line for any awards for excellence.

I *will* say that the camp authorities were pretty wide open about letting the inmates fill their time as they saw fit. It would have been wonderful if I had found myself in one of those luxury facilities where they have tennis courts and maybe a baseball diamond, but Camp George West was a little bit more blue-collar than that.

I did find a bright spot available among the camp activities, though. I've always loved to play horseshoes and they had about ten pits out in the back recreational area. No waiting. They had three concrete courts with nets and I played some pickup basketball (when I could persuade the other guys to let me play. I'm terrible at basketball.) Other than that, I just read books and did my assigned chores, and waited for the days to pass.

After I "graduated" from camp, I spent another sixty days in a halfway house far more restrictive than the camp had been. It was staffed with young guys and women who were allegedly planning to enter counseling as a career.

In theory, that seemed to point to them as the most likely candidates to offer a firm but understanding management staff to the facility. In reality, even though most of the women were all right, several of the guys were washouts from the police academy that hadn't made it because they had serious control issues. They were not monitored very well, and they had a great time by intimidating the residents. At least at the work camp, we had been allowed the freedom of the whole facility and unlimited time outside for activities, using the basketball courts and playing shuffleboard and horseshoes to help break up the monotony.

At LCTC (Longmont Community Transition Center), we were restricted to the building, *except* when we were out at a job which we were required to get as part of the rehab. We had minimal time to get to and from work so otherwise, we were stuck inside. We were always checked for drugs, alcohol, and other contraband when we returned to the facility, but the staff (particularly the guys) seemed to take special pleasure in doing extra rigorous checks for infractions of any sort on the inmates they didn't like. That included breath checks and pat downs. It didn't take much to get on their wrong side, either. Any complaining or signs of a 'bad attitude' and you would find yourself on the 'difficult' list. I don't have any solid proof of it, but it seemed as if the weekly chore assignments reflected those clients who were *in* or *out* of favor. Those on the list always seemed to draw the dirtiest jobs.

The only time we were allowed outside the facility was to step out into the alley behind the building where they gave the residents a fifteen-minute smoke break every two hours. I don't smoke, but even we few nonsmokers grabbed the fresh air while we could. That was the setup for every newcomer there.

If I remember correctly, it was possible to work your way up the ladder to obtain certain privileges after you'd been there for a while, but the two months I spent there wasn't really long enough to acquire that limited freedom. The funny thing is, the atmosphere at the halfway house was much worse than at the jail. There was more suspicion, more theft, and generally more tension at the place—and this was where they were allegedly trying to help you readjust to civilian life.

Since we were all required to find a job, I had the unfortunate opportunity to come face-to-face with a harsh reality. I suppose I shouldn't have been surprised, but there weren't a lot of jobs for people who were considered criminals, regardless of the nature of their offense. I ended up at a call center doing cold calls as a telemarketer. Frankly, that in itself borders on cruel and unusual punishment, both for the caller and the callees. I managed to sleepwalk my way through the sixty days without any major incidents, and after what seemed like an eternity, I was finally cut loose to go back into the real world.

Even though it felt like it had been an eternity, I had only been 'in stir' for about five months. After that relatively brief interruption in my life, I thought I had changed my behavior quite a bit. I was on the wagon again—at least for a few months, and I was trying to pay more attention to the world around me. I even got a library card. But the major change didn't happen until a few months later. The big alteration in my behavior came when I made the choice to refrain from driving when I was drinking. The fact that my driver's license was still suspended made that decision somewhat simpler. But the decision had to be made because, like before, I eventually went back to my old habits.

I had to get a bit more creative about how to obtain my liquor now, and found it easier than I thought. There were several liquor stores within a couple of miles of where I lived, and I chose one of three different ways to get there.

Once Mary went to work, I would choose my means of transportation. Occasionally, I would take my SUV and slip up to one of the stores and bring a bottle home. I knew I was breaking the law, but it didn't seem like that big a deal. I was very careful and I never drank before I drove. I was driving a very short distance to and from. And if I was feeling hung over or nervous about getting caught driving, I could get a taxi pretty inexpensively, or ride the bus. On a few trips, I walked to the store. The thing was, I was going to get my stash one way or the other.

I have to admit—and I may have a hole in my memory about this—but for some reason, I don't think I was mandated to take regular breathalyzers after my jail time. I suppose that's probably because I had 'paid my debt to society.' My sentence was finished, and I was an actual free man again. Even if I had been doing B.A.'s, as I said before, I had already worked out a (nearly) failsafe system of knowing just how much liquor I could handle and still come out clean for the checks.

The bottom line was a familiar one. After a few months of sobriety, I was back on the sauce. Once again, nothing in my pattern had really changed. Each day was following a routine I had fallen into not too long after I left Firefall for the second time in 1992, and my life had stayed totally stagnant for about seven long years. Just staying around the house doing nothing.

I read a lot and watched too much TV, and with Mary working full time, we didn't get out to socialize much. She and I were sufficient company for one another, and that was good as far as it went, but I think she might have enjoyed spending a girl's night on the town with a few of her friends from time to time. She may well have been staying close to home to keep me from indulging myself in my bad behavior too often or too much. I'm not sure. It was probably a good call on her part, because I tended to take advantage of my time apart from her to do my drinking, just like I did during her days at work.

And as for me, after all the years of traveling all over the world, I had become a complete homebody. I rationalized it as being the result of having had enough of that footloose, wanderlust style of life, but I was fooling myself. My real reason for being glued to my living room was that it was the easiest place to consume my eighty-proof buddy.

I know I've brought up boredom as an adversary a number of times, and said I would talk about it later. I suppose now is the time to discuss it. For me, boredom is the kiss of death. I can't stand it. It's crucial for me to have

Lame Brain

something worthwhile to occupy my mind. When I don't, I find myself desperately reaching for anything that will either fill the void or dull my senses to make me forget the need. And the ugly truth is, I was, myself, becoming a very boring guy. Probably the most exciting things that were happening in my life were the periodic trips to rehab every year or so. And as highlights go, that's setting the bar pretty low.

I looked at my recent attempts to beat my drinking habit and came to some disturbing conclusions. I had taken a shot at all those different rehab treatment centers without ever managing to keep myself on the straight and narrow. Despite my best efforts, the ultimate end was always the same. I would keep myself straight for a while after each additional stint, but as soon as the idle hours began to mount up and boredom kicked back in, it was only a matter of time before my sobriety was out the window. As a result, I was beginning to despair about finding any help from that avenue of pursuit.

It finally struck me that the problem wasn't so much that I didn't learn anything from the programs or didn't have the best intentions. It was just that once I was back at home, I simply couldn't figure out anything else to do. In hindsight, I guess I might not have been looking very hard.

From what I've been told, when you are training a puppy and you take away its toy, you should give it something else to concentrate on. I began to think that was what I was lacking. *A new toy.* A distraction. But try as I might, I couldn't find anything that stimulated my interest. *What I needed was a new obsession.*

My love of music hadn't totally faded or changed, but my *energy* for getting back into playing was not very strong. I'm not sure if it was fear that was turning me away from it, or something else.

Of course, the obvious answer is my habit, but I think there was more involved. You might ask what I had to be afraid of. In looking back, there were several possible things that might have been scaring me. It might have been my last few experiences (Roberts-Meisner and my re-affiliation with Firefall, as well as my stillborn solo run), none of which turned out to meet my expectations. In that case, it was a fear of failure. Then again, it might have been my recent inability to write anything I thought was very good. Or it might have simply been the magnitude of the task of trying to put something together again. All of those are things I—and almost every artist I've ever known—had to deal with, and overcome.

But what frightened me might have been the biggest and most unconquerable fear of all—the feeling that my best chances had passed me by. And knowing if that was the case, it was mostly because I screwed up the process with my irresponsible, self-destructive behavior. Or even if I couldn't bring myself to take the blame, that none the less, my best days were behind me.

Whatever the cause, music just wasn't the answer at that time, and with all that in mind, I decided that any more treatment was nothing but a waste of time and money until I found a new focus for myself.

Eventually, I did go back for one more stint at Westpines. It wasn't that I had changed my thoughts about what was missing in my mental set. I still suspected that rehab probably wouldn't help me. But I decided I was willing to give treatment one more go-round. It seemed worth a shot because now I had another hunk of information of what had to happen to make it work for me *after* I completed the program. I thought maybe putting my revelations in the counselors hands might make some difference.

I made plans to go in and talk to the counselors about my situation, and the effect that so many empty hours seemed to have on me. Unfortunately, the staff there was not able to provide me with any radically new ideas about what to do with my time. Naturally, they suggested that I try and find a job. But as I mentioned earlier, I had no marketable skills after spending my entire adult life playing music.

At the other end of the spectrum, I could very probably have gotten a job flipping burgers somewhere, but somehow I couldn't imagine that being a career choice that would contribute to my lasting sobriety.

I guess a few things crossed my mind to try, but most of them would also demand a large cash investment, and I wasn't really in a financial position to attempt anything like that. In the end, I spent a couple of weeks at the Westpines facility and then became an out-patient, driving to and from classes each day and sleeping at home. That stint helped me stay sober for several months longer than any of the others, not because there was any great breakthrough, but because by this time, I was even getting a little bored with alcohol itself. Go figure.

As the World Turns

Chapter Fifteen

Let me backtrack to the days after my incarceration. The months slid past, and before I knew it, it was already late 1999. I was astonished that that so much time could slip by me without my even noticing. Once I had completed my sentence, I stayed sober for a few months. But as usual, it didn't last.

Suddenly I found myself facing another New Year, and not only that, but also a brand new century and even a brand new millennium as well. One would think it would be a good time for reflection, and perhaps some really serious New Year's resolutions. It didn't work that way for me.

The symbolic value of what was taking place, time-wise, was totally lost on me. In my life, it was business as usual. I didn't even see it as an excuse to go on a bender, because in my world, any day was as good as any other to tie one on.

As far as resolutions went, I never bothered to make those. From what I've seen, very few people keep them, and I was already over my quota of broken promises.

My continued drinking was making my life more complicated all the time. Not because my lifestyle was any more complex, but because the intricacies of my thought processes were getting increasingly tangled up. I wasn't getting drunk every day, but more and more of my life was revolving around some aspect of my habit.

And in a very odd sort of way, I was beginning to overthink everything. Each of the elements in my life seemed to be pulling me in different directions, and I was having a lot of trouble making sense of it all. The main event was still the same, but the sideshows were getting out of hand.

For one thing, my tolerance for alcohol was so high that it necessitated a large outlay of money, and over a span of time it really began to add up. I knew I didn't have the luxury of piling more expenses on top of what was already there.

And there were other aspects that were becoming increasingly difficult to balance. Mary was closing in on fifteen years of sobriety, and that caused a growing sense of guilt in me. I wanted to be a full-fledged partner in her life, but as long as I kept drinking, I knew I was holding a piece of myself away from her.

There were also the matters of having to hide my liquor, keep my drinking a secret (as if), manufacturing situations that provided drinking time, and all the other little deceptions that go into being a practicing alcoholic with a healthy partner.

And then there was the inertia of my musical situation. I wasn't working on anything and there was nothing on the horizon. Hence, more time on my hands and a continuing unfilled need. That may sound as if it contradicts what I said in the last chapter, but it really doesn't. Even though I lacked energy to get going musically didn't mean I didn't miss it. It wasn't a blinding depression or something constantly on my mind, but somewhere behind my conscious thoughts was the feeling that something was lacking in my life.

I wasn't exactly drowning my sorrows, but I found it a lot easier to handle my frustration when I had a buzz on. The ultimate effect was that I didn't change anything, because I didn't truly want to. I was more or less emotionally paralyzed by having too many things that all needed to be dealt with, and therefore, I chose to deal with none of them. There's an old parable about the ostrich who sticks his head in the sand because he's unwilling to see the danger around him. I think it goes on to say it makes him feel like he's safe. That's a pretty good description of how I was conducting my life. I'm also pretty sure the ostrich winds up getting his ass kicked.

The whole routine had been going on for far too long, and the result was what I was talking about when I described the years I spent bouncing between sobriety, being back on the sauce, and inevitably finding myself in another rehab joint.

One of the most incredible aspects about that whole span of my life is the fact that Mary stuck with me through it all. I know I've mentioned that several times, but it's a thought that keeps coming to my mind even now, and it kept popping up back then, too.

Regardless of the generally subdued and unsatisfied tone in my account of these years, Mary was an ongoing ray of sunshine. She kept me laughing and enjoying myself through what would otherwise surely had been unbearable. Even though I write about how nothing was happening and nothing was changing, she kept my life from feeling anything like that. So as you read my less than exhilarating account of that phase of my life, please don't forget that there was a definite bright side to it all.

There were certainly some tense moments when I occasionally got over my own tolerance level and ended up smashed. I was doing almost all my drinking at home because as I said, I had decided not to risk any more legal problems or innocent lives by driving and drinking. Besides, when you're trying to keep a low profile about your drinking, public transportation, whether bus or taxi, doesn't work real well. Not to mention wanting to avoid spending too much time in the local bars.

Mary was working full-time, so I had a fair amount of liberty to do my drinking, but luckily, my behavior never changed that radically when I drank. You know, the 'nice' drunk thing. Still in all, I knew that *she* knew, and naturally she didn't like it. Most of my trips into rehab had been the result of agreements between Mary and me that were based on the undying hope that eventually I would get myself straightened out.

And so the days and months of the new year went by at a slow and steady pace with nothing really noteworthy happening. Before I knew it, another empty year had slipped away. Not the most dazzling way to usher in a new millennium.

If you consider this pattern I have just diagramed, it may not come as much of a surprise when I tell you that I really don't have anything at all to say or write about the whole year of 2001. It was basically just more of the same quasi-life that I had been living for several years. Maybe I was just getting ready for 2002, because a lot happened that year.

My last trip into rehab at Westpines took place in the springtime of 2002, and that, combined with the relatively long span of sobriety I managed to hang onto, occupied a good portion of that year.

In a reverse sort of way I take pride in the fact that my new awareness of my behavioral patterns kept me safe from some dangerous illusions. I didn't mistake the near-month of abstention I strung together before rehab for a signal that I was beating the problem myself. Even though I was able to put my usual behavior on hold for a while, I knew I was basically treading water and my sobriety was only temporary. By the same token, I admit I was proud of the fact I that could keep my habits at bay even for a little while.

By the late summer of 2002 after I had started drinking again, a very important thing happened, but I was too anesthetized to truly understand the ramifications of it. One afternoon while I was holding a glass I fell on my hand outside my front door. It caused a deep cut in my right palm. Mary was at work and I had had a couple of drinks too many. I just went inside and wrapped a towel around it and then sat down and held it up in the air. Thankfully it was late afternoon, so when Mary came in about an hour later, I was still bleeding and still drunk.

She took one look at me and said, *"WHAT HAVE YOU DONE?"*

I said it was just a cut, but she bundled me into the car and took me to the ER. They sewed my hand up, but we found out I had done ligament damage to my right index finger. I hadn't tried to call Mary at work, but I'm not sure whether it was because I honestly didn't realize it was serious, or because I knew I was high and didn't want to have to justify my accident as being nothing more than simply an accident.

I have had two operations on it since then, but I can still only bend my index finger about 90 degrees. And it wasn't until after the second operation that I could bend it that much. For at least two years, I couldn't even hold a guitar pick. Once I could hold one, it was another five years before I had enough strength in the finger to strum a guitar without the pick flying loose on the up strum, when the pressure is on that finger.

That incident made me totally unable to play any guitar, but it didn't stop me from drinking. And it probably should have. Guitar playing is a major part of my livelihood, yet losing the ability didn't strike me as important enough to take a closer look at how far astray my drinking habit had taken me. My perspective was badly distorted, if not lost completely, by my addiction.

There have been other factors which kept me away from my guitar from time to time, but that was the point when I stopped playing completely. It's hard to write songs when you can't play an instrument.

Just so as not to keep you in suspense, I finally picked the guitar back up about a year ago in 2014, and am finally starting to reestablish my playing ability. My skills are as yet no more than rudimentary, but I'm still a work in progress. And, strange as it might seem, in the last few years I have discovered that I can still write songs even without the benefit of my instrument.

How can I do that, you might ask? Frankly, it surprised me that I could. Over the years, a number of people approached me at concerts and said they were songwriters.

My first question was always "What instrument do you play?"

When they would answer that they didn't play anything, but just made up the words and the tunes in their heads, I would tell them that they weren't writing songs, they were writing poetry, or at best, tone poems. But now that I've been doing the same thing, I'm calling them songs. Why? Because after playing the guitar for forty years, when I compose the tune in my head, I know exactly what the chords are. Then I can just pick up my instrument and rough out the chords to make sure they match. So far they have.

Granted, I'm not nearly as prolific as I was when I had the guitar right there with me, and I don't get to make up my own chords. Nonetheless, I've written about six new songs in the last couple of years. That doesn't change the fact that I'll feel better about things when I'm able to use my guitar in the process again.

One Good Man

Now let's step back a few more years. But before I start this part of the story, I want to say something about the drinking thing. A lot of people with alcohol problems like to come up with reasons to explain why they began drinking. And they can be pretty creative about it. I've heard all kinds of stories, ranging from the absurd to the highly effective, but for the most part, they still fall under the heading of excuses.

One of the most popular categories are the stories about some difficulty that appeared in the person's life, and how drinking was the only way they thought they could handle it. As far as I can tell, there really isn't any good reason to *start* drinking when you are suddenly faced with a new problem. At that point, you can't even claim that your mind was fuddled with booze and you weren't thinking clearly. If you use your head, it's easy to see that alcohol won't *solve* anything. So using that as a reason for starting just doesn't hold up.

I might be willing to give more credence to those who were already drinking, and who say they stuck with the bottle to forget their problems. That, the bottle can do. But only temporarily, and then you just have to keep on repeating the process until you finally realize that all you're doing is postponing the time when you'll finally have to deal with the issue. It isn't going to disappear while you're out there on a binge.

The thing is, if you're already drinking a lot and a new problem appears, your head might not be clear enough to see that your booze will not only provide no answers, but will probably exacerbate the situation.

I think it requires a large amount of character to seize a moment of sobriety and sanity somewhere in there and realize that if you intend to find a solution to your dilemma, you need to straighten yourself up.

I evidently didn't possess that much character. When I was confronted by the IRS in 1982, my relationship with the bottle was already well established and the new trouble didn't really register as a game changer. At least not in the sense of a reason to stop my drinking.

By the autumn of 1993, my ongoing indebtedness to the government had already been an intrinsic part of my life for ten years. It was so ingrained in my annual routine that it had become a part of the scenery, in a manner of speaking. I didn't think about it. Let me rephrase that. I did think about it, but I simply accepted it as the way things were. It was just automatic that every month I wrote a check for $500 and every three months I added another check for $5,000.

But when I left Firefall again, money got a whole lot tighter. Then Mary and I had gotten hitched, and as I previously mentioned, the only money I was contributing was coming from my royalties with no new cash flow coming in from me at all.

Mary was working and contributing her money, but between the normal costs of living in Boulder (not an inexpensive proposition) and such things as car payments and various recreations, we were constantly faced with the possibility of coming up short.

I think in the midst of feeling that crunch we had some unexpected outside expenses and I had a couple of slim royalty periods, and I missed one of my $5,000 payments, and a month or two of the smaller ones, too.

Even though making the payments had been almost an unconscious reflex action, when times got tight, my instinct for self-preservation took control, and eating and keeping a roof over my (and Mary's) head seemed a lot more important than the IRS and my other bills.

You may remember that I made a passing reference earlier in the book (as well as subtitling this section) to the importance of "One Good Man" and told you I'd explain later. Well, I was about to meet him.

On a crisp afternoon in the early autumn of '93, I was sitting in my living room when a fellow in a suit appeared at my door. He was an older man, and I couldn't help but wonder why he might be coming around to my house. I think I felt vaguely uneasy as I looked through the glass panels of my door, because he had a very businesslike and somewhat official look about him.

Since I could see him, I knew he could see me, too, or I might have pretended no one was home. Therefore, because it was impossible to ignore him, I went to the door and asked what I could do for him. He said his name was Glenn Seward, and that he was an agent for the Internal Revenue Service.

I immediately felt a lot more than vaguely uneasy. Within about a split second I felt seriously sick to my stomach and a little dizzy. It didn't really make sense to try and play dumb, so I invited him in to sit down and asked him what was going to happen now that I had fallen behind on my payment schedule. He responded by asking me to tell him how this whole thing had gotten started.

So I took a deep breath and proceeded to tell him my story.

I started with how during the height of my touring days I had my taxes done by the band's business management and so on; how all I did was sign the forms when they were presented to me and from there I assumed the payments were being deducted from my accounts to be paid directly to the government. I had only found out much later that such had not been the case. The man I felt was responsible had not had any legal problems yet (although he was later brought up on charges of embezzlement from several major film stars), or at least none that I was aware of. As I told my tale, I was prepared for the usual skepticism I had always gotten from the representatives of the IRS. But Mr. Seward's reaction was not at all what I expected.

The other IRS agents I had dealt with when I was first addressing my indemnity acted like I was lying through my teeth, and had set out to cheat them from the start.

Mr. Seward, on the other hand, seemed as if he wanted to believe me, and said, *"That's a lousy way to get treated by the people you are employing to take care of you. I'll tell you what. As long as you're straight with me, I'll be straight with you, and I'll try to help you get this thing worked out. But if I catch you being less than totally honest, I'll cut you off in a minute, and you won't like what happens after that."*

I couldn't believe it. He changed my opinion of tax agents in an instant. He actually cared, and wanted to try and *help get me out* from under this whole thing. After that first meeting, Mary and I continued to work with Glenn, and over time we got to be very good friends, going to his home and meeting his family.

Although I had to keep paying my $500 and $5,000 payments for quite a while, at least I now felt like there was someone on the other side who was working with, rather than against, me.

Every government man I had been answerable to had made me feel like they were just waiting for an opportunity to catch me trying to pull a fast one. And I guess that's understandable. It's not unheard of to find an otherwise upright citizen trying to run a few numbers on those guys.

But you can be sure I was a hundred percent honest about every word I said to Glenn. You don't want to mess around and screw up a good situation when you're lucky enough to stumble into one.

2002, a Spacey Odyssey (The Conclusion of)

For the next ten years, Mary and I (as my wife, she was the unfortunate co-recipient of my indemnity) continued paying our monthly and quarterly dues to the government with no foreseeable end in sight.

The only difference was that on the couple of occasions when we were late with a payment, instead of facing the instant threat of the tax people swooping down on us with levies and greater penalties and punishments, we had Glenn Seward in there serving as a buffer to their wrath. He was able to keep things just flexible enough that we could catch up on the payment we had missed before any action was taken.

But then things changed radically. Glenn presented us with a most unexpected gift. He invited us to his office one day in 2002, and explained that now we were eligible to apply for an Offer In Compromise. He explained that by proposing and finalizing such an arrangement, we could put IRS debt to bed once and for all and simply pay normal taxes from that point forward.

He told us he would have brought up the Offer in Compromise earlier if it had been possible. He waited only because we hadn't met the conditions necessary for that kind of deal until then.

Since we had already paid in excess of *twice* the amount I had originally owed, I suspect it might also have had to do with the fact he was getting ready to retire and wanted to protect us from the possibility of being assigned to a 'tough guy' agent.

At the point in time when he made the suggestion, he made it clear that unless we could reach such a settlement, we would simply go on paying for the rest of our lives without ever clearing the debt. And he was absolutely right.

When I reviewed the figures, I discovered how much I had paid (a little over $600,000), and how little the debt had been reduced (hardly at all). It was easy to see that under the arrangement I was in, I could never clean the slate. The original debt was for approximately $241,000, and almost everything that had been paid so far had been eaten up by penalties and interest.

I suppose I had known all along that the figure wasn't diminishing to any noticeable degree, but it was such an unbearable truth that I couldn't bring myself to acknowledge it.

Until Glenn made the suggestion, I wasn't even aware that such a thing as an Offer in Compromise with the IRS existed. I was among those who chose to try and escape rather than deal with a situation, so the IRS dilemma had been one more thing I tried to solve by sustaining my alcoholic cocoon. It took one good man leading me by the hand to help me take care of the problem. And I'll forever be grateful to him.

* * *

Another major change took place late that year. Mary and I had been living at the same address for the entire twelve years we'd been together. We had weathered numerous highs and lows at that little house in back of Carolyn Maxwell's. Carolyn was our landlady and Mary's best friend.

At the end of 2002, she and her children decided that she would be better off in an assisted living situation. Having recently turned eighty-three years old, she was beginning to have an unacceptable amount of difficulty handling things on her own.

With Carolyn moving into her new circumstance, the property was going to be sold and our place would no longer be available to us. That meant we had to set off on a short-notice house search.

We had known for a while that such a day would eventually come, but we hadn't looked for a place because there hadn't been an immediate need. Carolyn was still a vital and lively little lady and as sharp as a tack. It was simply her physical limitations that dictated the move.

So in a way, even though in our minds we knew it was inevitable, in our hearts we were caught off guard.

After searching around as much as our limited time allowed, we ended up choosing a house in Longmont, a smaller town about ten miles northeast of

Boulder. It was partly choice and partly necessity because we needed to find something relatively quick, and property values in Boulder had gone through the roof. But Longmont was definitely different than Boulder, and we didn't look forward to moving to a place where we didn't know anybody and certainly couldn't claim any friends.

We soon accustomed ourselves to the situation though, and were adapting pretty well in spite of missing Boulder. That feeling was only an illusion, because what we really missed was what Boulder *used* to be, not what it *had become*. I'm not saying that Boulder was no longer a wonderful place to live, but it had changed greatly from the town we first came to love. And the thing we actually missed the most was our old, familiar, comfortable neighborhood.

Despite the uncertainty of our new situation, it didn't motivate me to step up and start getting myself together. If anything, my response was just the opposite. I still hung around without any real sense of direction about which way to go with my music or with anything else, only now I had a fresh excuse. I was a relative stranger in this new town and I hadn't figured out what might be around to attract my interest. So my solution was to stay at home, immerse myself (so to speak) in all my old familiar patterns, and not even bother to go check out what might be happening in the area.

I wasn't playing guitar, and I hadn't yet figured out that I could write songs without an instrument, so I wasn't composing anything. I didn't have any drive at all. I was just coasting along in an alcoholic haze and figuring—hoping—it would all work out.

The thing is, I *still* couldn't even grasp the fact that to have a moderately normal life, something was going to have to change dramatically, much less what the problem was. I look back in utter astonishment at how I could have so stubbornly refused to see what was right in front of me.

Of course I knew I was still a practicing alcoholic, but somehow I was unable (or unwilling) to connect my acknowledged alcoholism with any other problem in my life. I was totally oblivious to the ripple effect, and kept viewing it as a totally separate situation instead of something that permeated everything in Mary's and my life. The proper term for it is *denial*. I prefer to call it sheer idiocy.

There was one other odd element to my drinking by this point. I can never recall any situation during those years where I felt like I really *needed* a drink. On many occasions, I wanted one, but if I was otherwise occupied, I could get along for an unlimited amount of time with no liquor. Of course, in some cases I was aware that I would undoubtedly feel better if I had a drink or two. Those terrible hangovers. But those were the times I least wanted another drink, because I had learned that 'a hair of the dog' wasn't a hangover cure; it was just a postponement.

Even though I wasn't drunk all, or even most of the time, it's obvious that my brain was never anything close to clear, because I had absolutely no concept or plan for my life or for my family's future.

I know I did all of my trips to rehab before we made our move to Longmont, but I have to admit that a few of the stops in the middle years are a little hazy—at least in terms of their chronological order. I'm pretty sure about the last two I went through. The first of those was when I went to Parker Valley for the second time, and after that was Westpines Lutheran for a repeat performance. I mentioned before that Westpines was my last go-round with a clinic, and that I stayed sober for several months longer than with any other program I had been in. I also confessed to the fact that the boredom that lent itself so well to drinking had finally spilled over to boredom with drinking itself. But somehow I always managed to overcome that, and found my way back to the bottle again. I wasn't going to mention boredom anymore, but this was a different kind of boredom. I was bored with what I did when I was bored!

The More Things Change...

Chapter Sixteen

By the end of the summer of 2004, we had been in our Longmont house for almost two years. I found life in suburbia was not nearly as bridling the second time around as it had been when I first tried it in a suburb of Boulder during the '70s. For one thing, I was now a married man in my fifties as opposed to being a restless young single guy in my mid-twenties with an active career in music. Being married goes a long way towards calming a person down, and so does thirty additional years of time. I was anything but restless since we had moved from Boulder, and I have to say that 2003, the first year of our residency in Longmont, slipped past as uneventfully as 2001 had. And for me, just as vacantly.

There was only one important thing that happened during an otherwise uneventful 2003. And it wasn't a good thing.

It was early in the year, only a few months after we'd made our move to Longmont. I was living very quietly in the new neighborhood with the intention of keeping a low profile. All the "rules" I'd set for my drinking like staying at home when I drank were still in effect. But one night I ran out of liquor before I'd had enough to satisfy me. Even though I should have known better, I got behind the wheel after I'd had a few. Maybe it was a cosmic message to let me know I wasn't going to get any more slack from above, but this time the fates that had been so kind before suddenly turned against me.

I was obeying all the traffic laws, but I got stopped for having a taillight out. Naturally, the officer smelled liquor on my breath. He put me through the roadside tests and I didn't do well enough to slide through. After that, it was the same old song. Jail for the night, bail, and another court appearance. I'd used up all my brownie points a long time since, and this time they revoked my license. So now I got to deal with a new home in a new city with no wheels for the foreseeable future.

I knew certain things had carried over from my Boulder situation, such as the frustration of not being able to play guitar and my continued drinking. But as time went by, I began to see that the two were closely intertwined due to the growing aggravation of not being able to write songs, or at least not having figured out yet that I could. I kept on piling up lyrics in my mind, and I had no way to complete the cycle—by putting them to music.

Being without a driver's license, whenever I wanted to get out and about, it was either with Mary or in a taxi or on a bus. Since Mary was working full-time, my outside activities were somewhat limited. Needless to say, my old nemesis *boredom* was a frequent visitor, and my older pal *booze* was a constant companion.

When it came to drinking, the biggest aggravation was Sundays. I always tried to make sure I had at least a small stash of vodka (which had evolved into my drink of choice) on hand at home, but when I found myself getting low and it happened to be a Sunday when liquor stores weren't open to replenish my supply, I sometimes went out to the bars to do my drinking so I wouldn't tap out my home stock. That way, if I wanted to finish off Sunday night with a couple of drinks, I'd have it on hand. On the other hand, if my home stash was dry and I wanted more, it might have been inconvenient, if not impossible. I always tried to plan ahead.

Luckily, there were two or three restaurant-bars within walking distance, and since Mary worked most Sundays, it was easy to take a stroll down to the friendly neighborhood tavern and toss down a few rounds. As long as I didn't make a regular practice of it.

Strangely enough, after I finally got sober once and for all, Colorado voted to let liquor stores stay open on Sunday if they chose. If that law had been in effect then, it might have saved me a world of trouble.

One Sunday in autumn of 2004, all those particular circumstances that could send me out into the world to drink coalesced, and once again I broke my own rule of not driving when I knew I was going to drink. I didn't want to frequent the places near my home too often because as crazy as it sounds, I was trying to maintain some semblance of a respectable reputation in my neighborhood. The buses were only running at widely-spaced intervals, and there was a Chili's restaurant-bar about two miles away, so I decided to hop over there and have a couple of quick ones. I did just that, and then started to head back home.

I was not even close to being drunk when I left the restaurant, but I stumbled over a small pothole in the parking lot on my way back to my car. I didn't fall down or anything, but there was a family of diners on their way in who took it for granted that my misstep was the result of being under the influence. They went inside and had the manager come out and offer to get me a cab. I told him I wasn't drunk and declined the offer.

I knew I wasn't high. I also knew I didn't want to have to explain to Mary why the car was at Chili's and I was at home, or why I had been driving in the first place. So I told him my house was only a couple of miles away and I would have no trouble getting there. He said I did seem all right, but that the people who complained had said they intended to report me if I drove away from the restaurant. I thanked him and said I would be fine. Then I drove home without incident.

About three hours passed during which time I had two or three more drinks and exhausted my stash while I watched a football game on TV. At that point I had a pretty good buzz on.

Then the doorbell rang.

When I went down to answer it, I found two police officers standing there. They asked to come inside and I let them in (probably not my best decision). They told me they had been called because I had been reported for driving under the influence. The customers at the restaurant had reported me even though they had not even seen me pull out. (Later on, I was told that the bartender at the restaurant had said he thought I was definitely high, but when they asked him why he was still serving me, he changed his story and said he wasn't really sure.)

The officers asked me if I had been drinking since I got home, and in a knee jerk reaction, I said no. They told me I seemed pretty high and asked to see my license. When I showed it to them, they saw that it was revoked and arrested me on the spot, in my own living room. I was handcuffed and led out of my house and taken down to the station. One of the cops mentioned on the way out that it was interesting that I had done such a perfect job of parking my car. That seemed to surprise him, because he thought I had come home drunk.

I was charged with a DUI even though the police hadn't seen me behind the wheel. I tried later to tell them it was an automatic response and also a lie when they asked if I'd been drinking after I got home and I said I hadn't. They didn't believe me.

During the whole process, I was undergoing a wide spectrum of emotions. When the police arrived at my house, I was puzzled and naturally nervous. When they arrested me I went from puzzled to baffled. How could I be under arrest when no one had seen me drive? Isn't that only circumstantial evidence? And in my own home? When I was informed of what the bartender had said, anger kicked in. If he thought I was too high, why hadn't he said anything to me or cut me off? Finally, when I got sober enough to think about it fairly and acknowledged that I was driving on a revoked license, remorse made its appearance. Regardless of whether or not I had been in shape to drive home, I had broken the law in another way, so I didn't have a legal leg to stand on. I knew that when I faced a judge, I was probably in for a punishment more serious than anything I had been through so far.

I was right. The court didn't fool around this time. In the spring of 2005 I was convicted and sentenced to a year at the Colorado State Prison at Sterling.

Officially, I was to be in the minimum-security segment of the jail, but it certainly didn't resemble what I thought of as minimum security. My fellow 'minimum' prisoners were in for such crimes as kidnapping, rape, and murder. The guy across the hall had kidnapped and murdered his own eleven-year-old daughter, and the man down the hall had been convicted of committing multiple violent rapes! Those guys had worked their way from maximum to minimum by time served with good behavior. My cellmate was in for credit fraud, and there were other white collar criminals and non-violent drug offenders, but even compared to those guys, I was a less-than-intimidating addition to the cell block.

And it was *embarrassing*. It's one thing to be ashamed to let the other inmates in on the nature of your crime because it was so horrendous. It's something else when you don't want the word to get around because your crime was so wimpy. I didn't want the heavy-duty criminals making fun of me. Or deciding I might make a good girlfriend.

I was later told by one of my fellow inmates that the judge I went before was notoriously hard on alcohol-related offenses, but it was hard to believe I'd been arrested in my own home on circumstantial evidence for an offense that I'd only debatably committed to be sent away to a prison with an electrified razor wire fence around the yard. The fact of driving on a revoked license complicated things, but I'm still a little shocked at the way it all went down.

All these details notwithstanding, there was one essential truth at the root of my situation. My alcohol habit, and nothing else, had landed me in prison. A *real* prison.

I have to admit, I never felt physically threatened while I was there. It may have had something to do with a few guys around who recognized me from my music and kept me off the harassment list. I can't be too sure of that, because it was now almost twenty-five years since my more high profile days. But then again, some of those guys had been out of circulation for about that long, too, so to them, I might have still been news.

Mary presented me with my biggest worry. She told me the very first time she came to visit that the process she had to go through to get into the visitors room was terrifying.

She had to make a 250-mile round trip to come to Sterling, but she told me that was nothing. On the other hand, she said that it was almost a toss-up between how much she wanted to see me and how frightening it was to come in there.

I never saw what the prison looked like from the outside, but assuming it looked anything like the other state prisons I have driven past in the course of my travels, it must have scared the hell out of her before she ever got to the front gate.

I spoke to her on the phone every day and that was of course the high point of each twenty-four hours.

Other than that, prison life was exactly how they portray it in the movies.

The food was lousy, the exercise periods were too highly regulated, there were occasional fights between inmates, and at one point, someone smuggled some bad heroin into the maximum-security section, and three guys died. I think there was one escape, too, but the prison authorities try their best not to let that kind of news spread.

They offered a number of classes and training courses at Sterling, but every one of the interesting ones were booked solid and had lengthy waiting lists.

In the end, I was only there for about three and a half months and then they shipped me back to that same halfway house in Longmont (LCTC) for another ninety days. That's the way they do it in Colorado. After you are released from prison, you have to do a specified length of time in a halfway house to give you time to 'readjust' to society. I was now officially a felon, even though I'd always thought of myself as a fairly law-abiding citizen with a drinking problem.

I will admit that coming from a state prison made the halfway house seem not quite as bad as it had felt when I was there before. Don't get me wrong though; it was still just as repressive and depressing the second time as the first, and the same awful possibilities of bullying and favoritism were still in play. And there was still plenty of intimidation, suspicion, theft, and other types of the lower aspects of human nature on full display.

I also got a very thorough and all too sudden education about how I was perceived when I went looking for the mandatory job while I was at the halfway house. Every application had the same question about whether I had ever been convicted of a felony, and if so, would I explain.

They put that in there to be in compliance with the legal requirement that felons could not be discriminated against in the job market. That's what the law says anyway.

There was room for at most, one sentence for my explanation, and I doubt that anyone ever looked that far. When they saw the 'yes' marked under felon, they stopped reading. So once again I ended up in the netherworld of telemarketing.

…The More They Stay the Same

When I finally got back home, I was emotionally worn out. I was originally due to be on parole for a year, and even when I found out it was only going to be six months, I felt like I was running in place with no real purpose for the whole exercise. I felt a general malaise and a feeling of "Why bother?"

I was required to keep my job at the telemarketing place for the extent of my parole. It was in Boulder, which meant spending forty-five minutes each way on the bus, and making my wife come and pick me up at the bus stop nearest to home at 10:30 P.M. after every shift I worked. That was because the bus I took on the way to work that ran close to my home stopped running for the night long before my workday ended.

As I've mentioned before, telemarketing is not the kind of job that motivates one to aspire to greatness or carry a smile in their heart, so when I got home at night, I was probably pretty bad company for Mary. It didn't help that the salary for a job in that field is minimum wage. They did offer sales commissions, but the levels were almost impossible to ever reach, so the paychecks were miniscule.

Maybe I'm a glutton for punishment, but for a while I had two jobs, both in telemarketing. I was also dependent on Mary to take me to my regular breathalyzer appointments. Once again, I used my basic math to know how much I could drink and still consistently test clean. You guessed it. Despite all I gone through on account of my alcohol habit, I was still drinking. There's only one possible way to explain my behavior. And I didn't figure it out until long after I got sober. I let alcohol steal my will to change. It was easier to keep on doing what I was used to doing—even something so self-destructive—than to exert the effort to try for something better. I had turned into the ultimate passivist. That's right—I said passivist, not pacifist. I couldn't summon the mental energy to change myself or my lifestyle. I was totally passive.

I have had times in my life when everything fell into a certain kind of rhythm that was very enjoyable and even exciting. The rhythm it had fallen into now was totally mind-numbing. It was probably the most meaningless routine I can imagine being in, and certainly not consistent with the plan I had once had for my future.

The end of my parole period also signaled the end of my breathalyzers. That gave me a little more sense of freedom, and I expanded on that by saying goodbye to my mindless job(s). It's not as if I had any pressing plans or well thought-out goals, but I wasn't nearly as interested in deciding what I wanted to do as stopping what I didn't want to do. That was obviously not the best way to go about making any plans for whatever I might be thinking of doing. But it was the natural thing to do, considering I really didn't plan on doing anything at all.

I'm painting a very dark picture here, and it's the same picture that I'd been featured in for quite a long time. I was on the slow boat to absolutely nowhere. The only bright spot in my world at that point was Mary, whose patience and ability to see that something was still there in me kept her hanging in there through whatever else was going on around us. And she had a way of somehow keeping both our spirits up.

I only bring up her patience with me again as an update. I think most everyone eventually gets fed up when dealing with a problem that just won't go away. So I figure I should periodically mention that she was still there for me. She never stopped loving me no matter how hard my behavior must have been for her to endure. I sometimes ask myself whether I could have been as strong and as faithful if the situation had been reversed. I don't honestly know if I would have been that forgiving or that brave.

What was even more astonishing is that she did this when her own job situation had gotten a lot trickier. Since leaving her position at Charles Schwab stockbroking firm, none of the positions she had found had kept her attention or been equal to her considerable abilities, but she continued to hold things together as she looked for the right position.

We had been experiencing problems with unknown parties hacking into our computer ever since we had made the move to Longmont, and for quite a while, we tried to chalk it up to the area where we lived. There were a large number of computer savvy people formerly employed by nearby software companies who lived in our immediate neighborhood. Evidently someone (or more than one someone) among them thought riding someone else's system for free was thriftier than paying for such services themselves.

As time went by and we kept going through hard drives much faster than was normal, we could no longer just shrug it off. Having to regularly replace our equipment was getting very expensive. We tried going to our service provider, who sent us to the sheriff's department, who said it was out of their jurisdiction and sent us to the local police.

There, the police said that they could see that something was going on, but computer intrusions were not their strong suite. They told us they were best at tax evasion and child pornography. We told them that we couldn't use them in those areas. That's when they sent us back to our service provider. Round and round she goes, and where she stops, nobody knows.

By late 2005, the intrusions on our computers had become a sizeable problem and were interfering with Mary's search for a good job. On several occasions, she sent out her resume got no response, even for positions for which she was ideally suited. This was, of course, not only disappointing, but also very puzzling. She knew she had all the necessary skills and references, but no one even seemed interested enough to call back. When she tried calling some of the companies to follow up, she discovered her applications had never arrived at their destinations and they had no idea who she was. Somewhere along the line, her applications had been diverted to somewhere unknown.

The intrusions also made it impossible for her to take a couple of online courses she had been interested in.

I keep saying "our" computers, but that's not how it was. At that point in time, I had never once so much as sat down in front of a system, nor would I for several more years. So I wasn't any help there. Mary, on the other hand, was very technically advanced and had seen more than her share of the dark side of computer use when she worked for Charles Schwab. Having worked in the fraud section, all she was exposed to were the miscreants and scam artists using the Internet to rip people off. With that background, she was very sensitive to irregularities in our own system.

But she couldn't figure it out either, so we just kept dealing with it the best we could and trying (with no success) to find some help from the sources that should have been able to trace the problem.

Unfortunately, it hadn't been realized yet just what a huge monster computer hacking and identity theft in all its forms was at that time, or the world-wide scourge it would eventually become.

So guess how I chose to deal with it? I had a few drinks. Daily.

As 2005 drew to a close, my life had gotten pretty close to a dead stop. What I was doing was a lot closer to *existing* than living, because I had no plans and very few activities. I read a lot and watched an excessive amount of television.

Since I wasn't driving, I didn't have the tools to go out and invent something to occupy my time, nor did I have much interest in just popping out to see what was going on.

I have seen some people rationalize doing nothing by claiming to be looking for hidden truths or answers to the eternal mystery of life. Not me. I was just channel surfing to find a good movie on cable.

Mary had been working for Verizon for about a year, but once I had finished with my legally-mandated work in telemarketing, I was willing to just sit back and wait for my next royalty check. In retrospect, I'm not proud to acknowledge the person I had turned into at that point. I had spent my whole life pursuing goals, and now I was acting like an invertebrate slug. I think I had put my brain in neutral along with everything else.

I knew something had to change, but I'd already known that for a long time. I just didn't know where to look for inspiration, and I guess, I didn't try too hard to find any. Music was not an option, because of my damaged hand, or at least that's what I told myself. I wasn't even drinking as much as I once had, because I wasn't getting high anymore.

So the weeks and months went sliding by, and I watched the whole thing as a spectator. Maybe the scariest thing is that I hardly even noticed. But what I didn't know was that there was something on the horizon that might not have been the path back to real life that I would have picked as my first choice, but which certainly provided me with the motivation I had been lacking. It also monopolized my attention and made my life very one-dimensional for the next three years. Come to think of it, one-dimensional is better than zero-dimensional, so maybe it was an improvement.

Changing Horses

Chapter Seventeen

As 2006 began and I looked ahead, I figured my life was probably going to be just about the same as it had been since I finished my parole. However, I did begin to notice one small change that had been quietly coming on for the last several months. Believe it or not, my drinking was actually starting to tail off. I said at the end of the last chapter that I wasn't drinking as much because I wasn't getting high anymore, and I have to believe that was one of, if not the major contributing factor to my slowdown. I mean, if I couldn't even get a little buzz going, what could possibly be the point? There was also the ever-present (dare I say it) boredom factor, but as I recently noted, now it was boredom with drinking itself.

I'm not trying to say that the alcohol didn't have any effect on me, but I was definitely getting the short end of the stick on the deal. I would have a few drinks without getting a buzz (even though I'm sure my external appearance and actions were just as impaired as ever) and then drink some more and go straight to being plastered. I had lost the (allegedly) enjoyable middle ground that had always been the desired goal. And I still had to endure the hangovers. All that was left over was the habit. So with that dubious set of motivations, I found I was no longer drinking every day.

The first four months of the new year went by with no surprises. I sat around waiting for something to happen, and not really expecting that anything would. Up until the very first week of May, my life slipped by in much the same manner, but then the fun (?) started.

I've already described how on the morning of Saturday, May 6th, I walked down my hallway, oblivious to the fact I was about to come foot to rug with the unlikely arbiter of my future for the next few years. Of course, I'm speaking of the sharp corner of our kitchen island, which I was about to introduce to the left side of my forehead.

As I explained in the second chapter, our puppies had chewed up an ink pen and spotted the carpet. In order to camouflage it until we could get it cleaned, we had put down a throw rug over the effected spot(s). I had tangled my feet in the rug and tripped, stumbling directly into the sharp corner of the island.

After reading the last several chapters, one would no doubt assume that I was either drunk or hung over, but that was not the case. My drinking had gotten to be less of a full-time pursuit, and just by chance I hadn't had any alcohol either that morning or the day before. I just wasn't watching my feet as I walked, and the pups had already roughed up the little rug I encountered. Ironic, don't you think?

I don't need to offer a play-by-play account of the next eight days, since nothing out of the ordinary happened until my Mother's Day trip to the hospital and the attending physician's dire predictions for my future walking abilities, but I think I should fill in the month between that visit to the ER and the day the predictions came crushingly true.

Maybe it had to do with my lightening up on booze, or maybe it was because of the medical warnings, or maybe it was just because it was springtime again. For my money, it was more likely a combination of all three.

So, for whatever reason, I suddenly seemed to have a lot more energy than usual, and during the remainder of May, I found myself out and about more than I had been since we moved to Longmont four years previously.

I started riding the buses to several different destinations on the days when Mary was working, and going out together with her just to ride around when she was off work. Occasionally, I got adventurous and caught a bus into Boulder to see what was going on, grab lunch at some old haunt, or to get together with one friend or another.

I even found myself going out for walks, sometimes with Mary and the puppies, and other times alone. There are a lot of songs that speak of springtime in the Rockies, and there's a very good reason for them. You don't actually have to be doing anything in particular, or going anyplace special to enjoy what nature and the surroundings have to offer.

So on that day when I took a direct route from my bed to the floor, it was a little bit more distressing than it would have been a few months earlier. I hadn't exactly been turning into a man about town, but I was at least a little bit active, and for me *that* was a big step forward.

Back in chapters two and three I talked about my attitude regarding my injury in the following months, and the false starts towards getting into the therapy before I finally went for it. But to make things clear, I think I should cover the same time period from a different perspective here, and describe what else was going on in my head and in my life.

It's fairly ridiculous for me to say that I felt *imprisoned* by my new limitations; because the only difference in my behavior was that I suddenly had no choice about sitting around all day. Even if things had been changing slightly for the last month, all that had really happened when my mobility disappeared was that

Lame Brain

I had returned to the routine I had been adhering to for several years before that. But that's the way I felt. Imprisoned.

As far as I was concerned, it was a tremendous alteration in the state of things from when I had formerly *chosen* to do nothing, to when I was now *forced* to do nothing as a result of my condition. So it was back to the old TV set and reading whatever I could put my hands on to occupy most of my waking hours. It's a lucky thing (relatively speaking) that it was the middle of the baseball season. I've been an Atlanta Braves (and before that, Milwaukee Braves) fan since 1957, and at least they played baseball nearly every day.

And guess what started to take an upswing again? But the funny thing is, I didn't start to drink a larger amount, because I still wasn't able to get that old time buzz. I just drank more regularly, as in almost every day when Mary was at work. By consuming less volume, I managed to avoid most of the hangover-inducing episodes. I still occasionally indulged too much in the vain hope of getting high, but for the most part it was just something to pass the time.

And when I did overdo it, I truly paid the price. The hangovers seemed to be bigger, longer, and generally worse than I remembered. Maybe it was because I wasn't getting even minimal exercise to help dissipate the poison.

I was also facing a whole new set of challenges as far as obtaining my booze. On a very infrequent basis, I would ask Mary to take me to a liquor store, but that was a rarity. Of course she was dead set against me drinking, but as I have said before, she knew that the only way I would permanently quit was when *I and I alone* made up my mind that quitting was what I *really* wanted to do. In the meantime, she was hoping to keep some sort of balance between not wanting me to drink, and not wanting me to put myself in harm's way by trying to get my alcohol myself.

As a result of wanting more liquor than those rare occasions that Mary's help could provide, I chose some very ugly ways to feed my habit. And since I use that term, I want to say that never once in my entire drug-using career did I stoop to some of the embarrassing depths I went to with booze.

There was a liquor store in our neighborhood, and once Mary had gotten me a wheelchair, I actually wheeled myself down there on several occasions to buy a couple of bottles. I had no compunctions about buying in volume so as not to have to make the trip more often than necessary. More than once, I had liquor delivered by taxi. The grocery store we frequented had a liquor store next door, so when I took a taxi down for food, I always made sure to make the extra stop. Since I was wheelchair bound, the driver would usually go in and get my bottles for me.

The one thing I never did was to ask a friend to bring me a bottle. In some odd way I thought that doing something like that would be a blow to my dignity and my reputation. Think about it. I had been in jail twice, been through seven or eight different rehab programs, and took a wheelchair to the liquor store, but asking a friend to bring me a bottle would somehow cause me an embarrassment I couldn't endure. And the idea that my reputation was even a consideration is even harder to believe. As the saying goes, I'm pretty sure that ship had long since sailed.

Aside from going out to the market now and then, or when I needed to make a trip to restock my stash, I didn't spend too much time away from my house. It was somewhat different when Mary was not at work, and then we made a point of getting out of the house as much as possible. But it wasn't my doing. It was Mary. I credit her for being the spark plug to get us out and about, because my injury had put a damper on my desire to go much of anywhere.

She had an easier time convincing me to step out once baseball season was over. But not so long after that, we started to be more reliant on the whims of the weather. Anyone who has spent time around the Front Range area of Colorado knows how fickle the weather in autumn can be. One day it'll be in the 70s and the next it will have dropped forty degrees and it's snowing like crazy. So we just had to play it by ear and go when the going was good.

Soon after that, I started to work my way around to the mindset that eventually led me to get going with my recovery. First, there was the search for the proper facility. Then, the false starts at therapy. They tended to be the punctuation points for whatever else was going on in my life. Of course I was still drinking on Mary's workdays, but on the days she was home I usually stayed away from the bottle. That made it a little easier to at least try to start a therapy program.

Still in all, the months meandered by in an aimless sort of way, and nothing of value got done. In hindsight, I can see it had to have been driving Mary crazy. She was doing all she could to motivate me into making the right moves and start working my way back to health, assuming it was possible. But that took participation and I was still dragging my feet.

My internal feelings weren't even clear to *me* as to why I was hesitating, so there was no way I could explain it to *her*. She was totally in the dark and doing the best she could. The vacuum I created by my hesitation pretty much stymied any real change for us to look forward to anymore.

It wasn't until way after the fact that I realized somewhere in the back of my mind the real obstacle to making a commitment to start some program of recovery was that then there would eventually be a resolution to the situation. In other words, if I actually agreed to participate in the game, sooner or later I would have to be a winner or a loser. Deep down, I was afraid I might be the loser. On the other hand, as long as I refused to start to play, I wouldn't be faced with an outcome.

So, with the exception of that tiny alteration represented by not spending my whole life in my living room, and at least looking like I was going to make a move to try and repair myself, that's the way it continued for the time between June of 2006 and September of 2007, when I finally got serious with my attempt to get the use of my legs back.

I can't really say whether I might have adjusted myself to what had to be done any more quickly than I did if I had been alcohol free. There were a lot of diverse things going on in my mind during that span of time, and as powerful an ingredient as booze might have been, I don't believe that taking it out of the equation would have changed the overall curve of my recovery that much.

And there's a reason for it. Alcohol has a way of magnifying most emotions. So while it may have increased the stubborn way I fought against bending my ego and giving in to the notion that I had to accept therapy if I wanted to get better, it also made me just as stubborn about getting it done when the time came that I realized there was no other way.

Once I actually started my serious efforts at recovery, that obstinate attitude stuck with me like a different sort of hangover. As if my mind was saying, "I'll be damned if anybody's gonna' tell me I can't walk again!"

Concerning Old Dogs and New Tricks

Chapter Eighteen

A funny thing happened to me early on in my rehabilitation therapy. I finally stopped drinking once and for all. After so many unsuccessful attempts and rehab programs had accomplished exactly nothing, and two stints in jail had failed to wise me up, it was a bad medication situation that finally turned the trick. As I've said before, by the end, I was mostly drinking for lack of anything better to do. But after I had sustained my injury, having "nothing better to do" occupied a lot of my time.

I have mentioned that even though Mary made it clear she didn't like my drinking habits, she also knew the only one who could stop me drinking was *me*. We both knew I was still drinking in the days since my accident, so with that in mind it was clear that we would have to come to some mutually acceptable arrangement with me being totally housebound. And eventually we did.

By way of a compromise, I gave control of my liquor over to her. It was more of a sacrifice for her than it was for me, because she would have felt so much more peace of mind if I had been willing to just stop altogether, whereas I was only eliminating the hide-and-seek aspects of the situation and the difficulty of mixing my own drinks. Plus, since everything was out in the open now, I no longer had to battle through all the gyrations of obtaining my alcohol in the first place.

Our arrangement was that she would mix up a pitcher of my favorite libation, which at that point was a "Cape Codder" (vodka and cranberry juice), and leave it in the refrigerator when she went to work. Then, when I wanted a drink, I didn't have to struggle through making it myself.

The positive angle for her on this was that she was now in control of the strength of the drink, and only she knew where the alcohol was. And last, which we both knew, she was able to water down the vodka. In those last days when Mary got home from work, the pitcher was usually still full, plus there was often a large part of my first drink remaining in my glass. But I was still imbibing some amount every day, no matter how small, so it wasn't really a victory at all.

My injury took place just before Mother's Day of 2006, and I finally went into a serious attempt at therapy sixteen months later in September of 2007. I was still drinking as it neared the end of 2007. That's when things went in a whole new direction. There were several factors involved in that change.

Headed for a Fall

Let me start at the beginning and lay the groundwork for the situation. One afternoon during the winter of 2001, I was carrying some groceries up the walkway to my front door. We had a series of flagstones leading to the house, and on this day they were covered with about an inch of snow. The concept of permafrost and the fact that it plays havoc with frozen earth was outside my area of knowledge. I didn't realize things like flagstones that are embedded in the ground can rise slightly during a hard freeze.

I caught my toe on one of the concealed stones and went down heavily on my knees but I kept my groceries from spilling. I knew I had hit the stone pretty hard, but it was very cold and I didn't feel any pain. I just ignored it and finished my trip inside. Once I got warmed up, my knees hurt plenty!

When I woke up the next morning with an ankle that closely resembled a softball, I figured I must have somehow damaged it when I fell and had been too focused on how much my knees hurt to notice.

I called my PCP (Dr. David Luce) to get it looked at and make sure it wasn't sprained. I went to his office and got him to check it. He told me that he didn't think it was sprained; that I should go to the hospital and have an ultrasound on it to be sure.

I went to hospital and did as he suggested. Then I went out to the waiting room until they could process the test and give me the results. While I was sitting there, a phone call came for me. It was Doctor Luce, who told me in a very stern voice to check myself into the facility right away.

I said, "For a sprained ankle?"

He laughed and said, "You should be so lucky!"

It seems the ER physician had discovered that I had a blood clot extending almost the entire length of my left leg from the ankle to the thigh. The shape of the clot was by itself a major shock to me. I'd always been under the impression that clots were little ball shaped things like a BB or a miniaturized marble. Finding out my whole vein could be blocked was a nasty surprise. So my doctor's advice was to get my little rear end into the hospital and don't take a lot of time doing it.

There was only one little problem with that. *Me.*

The thing is, I've always been consistent in my behavior towards hospitals.

When I say consistent, I mean consistently stupid, so I told him I had some things to take care of later that afternoon and I would check in the following morning.

Boy, did he get mad. He yelled and even cursed a little, which was definitely not his style, and told me I would be an incredible idiot if I didn't check into the hospital right then.

Evidently, when a blood clot as big as mine is found, it's important to get immediate care. Even one day could make the difference as far as the clot breaking up and causing a stroke or a heart attack. When I finally checked in, they made me *very* aware of that fact. With a big smile, I promised I would *never, ever* let it happen again. They were not amused.

I spent a couple of days at Boulder Community Hospital while they dissolved the clot and inserted a "green screen" in through my crotch. That device is a little doo-dad that eventually resides in the lower part of your chest. It prohibits any future clots from breaking up and going to the heart or the brain. They also put me on a blood thinner to try and prevent any further clotting events. That's why, when my blood blister broke on that fateful Mother's Day, I figured it would be a good idea to lie down in the hallway where my blood would be flowing away from my wound.

Just so it doesn't catch anybody off guard later, I should mention that just as a general policy (one that had its start back in the early years of the new millennium), Doctor Luce and I had decided it would be a good plan for me to do a blood draw about every six months, so we could monitor my blood pressure and my health in general. After every draw, we would go over the results and make any adjustments.

Since I wanted to keep some track of my situation, and I was still imbibing, my first question to him after each draw was to ask how my liver looked. The answer always came back the same; my liver appeared to be fine. My trust in that information would be the source of a very dramatic surprise a few years later.

I know David would rather not have kept finding that my organs were completely healthy because he hated my alcohol abuse and he knew I couldn't be as well off as I seemed, no matter what the reports said. He told me more than once that if I didn't quit, I was going to die. And soon. But I'm getting sidetracked.

About the same time as I had the blood clot, I had a series of seizures, which persisted for a little over a year. Doctors tested me for epilepsy and came up with inconclusive results. To provide me with a modicum of safety, they added an anti-seizure medication to my blood thinner, and over the next few years the specific one they prescribed was changed about three times to accommodate what my needs were perceived to be.

Eventually, I was put on Tegretol. This specific medication was, at that point, relatively new, and had only been approved by the FDA for a little while before I started taking it. It turned out that there were a few things about the drug that hadn't shown up yet. For most people, Tegretol is a very effective aid in seizure prevention. For a minority of others, the drug works fine for a span of time, sometimes up to a year, without any adverse side effects. Then without any warning, it becomes a contra indicant on many other common meds. I was one of those people.

In researching for this book, I have been made aware of numerous other rather undesirable side effects of the drug, but none of those came into play with my situation, so I'll refrain from trash talking about it, except as it related to me.

Three months after I started therapy and a day or two before Thanksgiving of 2007, Mary started noticing I was much less talkative than normal. I would sit around, which was of course standard operating procedure at that point, but she thought I seemed even more listless than usual. On Thanksgiving Eve, I was in the living room when she came in from the kitchen to ask what side dishes I wanted for turkey dinner, besides the usual ones. I didn't respond, so she asked again. Again, no answer.

The third time she asked, I suddenly snapped my head around at her and yelled, *"WHAT DO YOU WANT FROM ME, WOMAN?"*

I don't remember any of this, but that was definitely not the way I talked to my wife. Ever. It was so much not my style that Mary immediately called Steve, who was my caregiver at the time. When he came over, the two of them managed to manhandle me into the car and take me directly to the ER, knowing something was drastically wrong.

The people at the hospital put me in ICU, where I stayed for seven days. I wasn't fully rational for the first day or two. When they asked me my age I was convinced that I was forty-six. I was able to tell them my accurate birth year and day, and also what year it was. They told me to do the math. The math said I was fifty-eight, so I spent the next two or three days wondering what in the hell happened to the last thirteen years of my life.

When I did a little more math later on, I discovered that forty-six and thirteen don't add up to be fifty-eight. So I guess my head was only getting clear a little bit at a time. After about four days, they were ready to let me go, except for one small thing. The blood samples that were routinely taken did identify the culprit as the Tegretol, but the lab also found an inordinately high amount of ammonia in my bloodstream, and couldn't explain why. My doctor also didn't like it, so I stayed put.

The primary physician on my case was Dr. Charles Van Hook, and about the fifth day I was there he brought in Dr. Robert Dolan, a gastroenterologist friend of his, when he walked his rounds. Dr. Van Hook wanted to see if Dr. Dolan could shed any light on the mysterious ammonia.

When they came to my room that day, Doctor Dolan took one look at me and said, "You drink quite a bit, don't you?"

I told him I didn't drink nearly as much as I used to.

He countered by asking, "How much did you *used to*?"

I answered, "A lot."

He immediately scheduled several tests for me, including removing fluid from the area next to my stomach. I've never been in the medical field and so I'm not sure if you're supposed to *have* fluid next to your stomach in the first place, but I did.

The next day Doctor Dolan came back with the results and said he had some important things to tell me, the most important of which was that I had about 10% of my liver functioning.

It seems that unless they are specifically testing for it, a normal blood draw won't reveal the type of liver damage that I had. I must admit, that was kind of a big blow after having all those misleading good reports from the blood draws. I had been living with the illusion that I was somehow getting away with my abuse, and suddenly I'm informed that I'm about a half step from either a mandatory liver transplant or an early exit from life.

Doctor Dolan told me that rule number one was I could never ever have another drink. Considering my attitude about alcohol at that point, the news was not particularly devastating. The main thing it did was offer me a reasonable excuse not to drink anymore. And since any single factor that would have tipped the scales either way could have determined my behavior, I suppose it was a good thing overall that the unbalancing item went towards sobriety. What I'm trying to say is at that point, I didn't really care about drinking one way or the other, so it was no problem to go with the flow, and accept the doctor's orders.

I sort of stifled a mental yawn and said, "Okay, but you said you had something else important to say other than my liver results. What is it?"

He thought I must not have understood his news, so he said, "No, I mean you can *never* have any more alcohol."

I said, "*I GET IT!* No more liquor. Now what's your big news?"

Doctor Dolan shook his head and left the room.

They kept me in the hospital for three more days, but at least they moved me out of ICU and into a normal ward. The only additional problem I had was a steady loss of weight during my entire stay. I dropped about ten pounds during the week and a half I spent there. That's about a pound a day, and I probably would have been more alarmed if it hadn't been a problem for which I already knew the three causes. Number one, alcohol is very fattening, and that had been removed from my diet. Number two, the hospital food, while healthy, was nothing to write home about in terms of taste. Number three, you don't get to do a lot of midnight snacking in a hospital bed. Once I was home again, the weight loss stopped dead and I slowly recovered the missing poundage by going back to my old eating habits.

Lame Brain

Doctor Dolan scheduled me to take various tests several times in the ensuing months. These were taken at increasing intervals of time to monitor the progress of my liver as it was regenerating itself. I still can't help but be tremendously grateful that the liver is the only organ in the human body capable of renewing itself, if given a chance.

The first set of tests was two weeks after I went home. The next, a month after that, then a three-month gap, and finally, a whole year. On the last visit for test results, the good doctor told me that for my age, I was probably in better shape than he was. Even though I knew he was only trying to bolster my confidence, and the statement was not exactly something I should accept as gospel truth, it still felt nice to hear that my organs were on the comeback trail.

And that is the story of how I stopped drinking. I have never drunk another drop of alcohol since that hospital visit, and I really don't miss it.

I can honestly say that not only have I never had any cravings, I have never even experienced the common phenomena of drinking dreams. That may be because I did have a chronic drinking dream while I was still on the bottle. I used to have this nightmare where I was getting ready to go on stage for an outdoor stadium show, and I was so drunk I had to crawl to the side of the platform and then be helped up the stairs. When I got up there, I had to cling to my microphone stand to keep from falling down. And when the first song started, I drew a complete blank on the words. That's when I usually woke up in a cold sweat.

I don't suggest that anyone use my example of how to kick the habit, because if it hadn't been for the unlikely set of circumstances that all fell together at just the right time, I probably would have walked right into a very early grave still convinced that I was getting away with my ongoing alcohol abuse.

And consider for a second just how long the odds are for all the contributing elements to have come together. First, there was the fall on the stone that led to the accidental tests and discovery of the blood clot. That led to the blood thinner. If not for that, the Tegretol wouldn't have had anything to contraindicate with, and I wouldn't have ended up in the hospital where they noticed the mysterious high ammonia reading. There would never have been any tests to reveal the shape my liver was really in, and I would have gone right on drinking until I had completely run my course. That's not a trifecta I'd be willing to bet on.

I should add that it probably isn't a really good idea to wait until you're bored with drinking before you try to quit. A lot of people don't get bored as easily as I do.

And finally, I think I should also mention that at that juncture they took me off any seizure medication, and I have never had any seizures since. I am convinced I never suffered from epilepsy. I think I might have had alcolepsy, though.

There's Just One More Thing…

Chapter Nineteen

While I was talking about my brain injury earlier in this book, I described a lot of the exercise routines and regimens that contributed to the progress of my recovery. Time-wise, I carried my dialogue a little past the point when this next bit of information came to my attention.

It didn't dawn on me at first that besides the loss of being able to walk, which tended to dominate my attention for some time, there were other things I would have to work on to recover—the biggest of which was balance. I had always had excellent balance, and now I had very little. When you can't walk, balance doesn't really come into play that much, so it's only natural that I hadn't noticed. As I recovered muscle tone and strength in my legs, more and more of my rehab was focused on regaining my lost equilibrium. There were some other things I wasn't really prepared for, either.

Besides cracking my head open, I've sustained a number of injuries over the years. One thing they have usually had in common was that the treatment for each injury was predictable, and the healing process was pretty linear. The same thing has held true for almost all of my injuries with the exception of a few back problems.

With brain injuries, all bets are off. One day everything is coming along fine, and the next day you're suddenly back where you were weeks ago. It's not only confusing, but it weighs on your spirit and your stamina. And it eats away at any confidence you might begin to build about the outcome of all your work.

When I finally started my serious efforts at recovery and was faced with those setbacks, I silently asked the question—and more than once, I might add—whether I was fooling myself about regaining the use of my legs. I would briefly consider tossing in the towel and accepting the fact that this was how it was going to be. Me and the wheelchair, from here on. But something kept nagging at the back of my consciousness telling me I shouldn't give up hope. And I knew there was some reason, but I couldn't think what it could possibly be.

Then one day it hit me. It was because of my father and what had happened to him.

While I was growing up, my family lived on the Gulf coast of Florida. The Roberts' had been in Clearwater since the late 1800s, and were serious water people. They loved to do anything around the water, including boating, swimming, snorkeling, and water skiing. In fact, my great grandfather was among the first aquatic mailmen anywhere. He used to deliver the mail from Miami around and up and down the west coast of the state by boat way back at the turn of the last century.

Anyway, once my memory of the whole event came back to life, I realized what it was that had been tugging at the back of my awareness. I suddenly remembered that when I was little more than a baby, my dad had a close encounter with a mangrove island that nearly crippled him permanently.

If you've never spent any time down in that part of the country, you may not know what mangrove islands are. They're not really islands at all, but simply clumps of trees that put down roots in the sand at the water's bottom. Those 'islands' dotted the waterways all over Florida, and were fairly common in between the mainland and the Channel Islands along the West coast of the state. They looked harmless enough, but they could be very dangerous to the uninitiated.

The main hazard was and is that the roots also spread out from the edges of the islands just under the surface of the water and can't be seen from above until you're almost right on top of them. The extended roots quickly get covered with oysters, complete with their razor sharp edges. They can cut up anything that comes in contact with them, and they do it with a vengeance.

When I was about three years old, my dad was out water skiing with some friends. The guy who was driving the boat was either not very capable or not paying much attention, and evidently didn't understand how it worked with those islands. One way or the other, while my dad was the one on the water, the driver steered him too close to one of the mangrove islands.

My father saw a big root stretching out just ahead of him and tried to signal the driver to change course, but the guy didn't see him and kept his course straight and steady. My dad had no choice but to drop his ski (he was slaloming) and try to dive over the root. He managed to clear it except for one of his legs. I don't remember which one, because after the whole event was over, it was never talked about again in the family. That's one reason it took me a while to pin the memory down.

His leg was sliced to ribbons and if I'm not mistaken, he took somewhere in the vicinity of seven hundred stitches. I know that sounds like an incredible amount, but they had to stitch several layers of flesh starting at the bone. I do know they took a quart of oyster shell out of his leg.

As I said, I was only three so I'm a little hazy on some of the details, and since my mom and dad have both passed away I can't go to them for information. I can't say for sure how long he was in a wheelchair, but I do know they told him it was questionable whether he would ever walk again, and if he did, he would be on crutches.

But I also remember by the time I was seven, he ran me down at a picnic one day when I tried to beat him to the fried chicken!

With that memory as a clear and heavy-duty motivator, I made up my mind that if he could do it, so could I. Family bonds are powerful things, and powerful memories last a long time.

Some Truths Can Be Hard to Speak…Or Hear…

I found out that certain things I never would have imagined to be effected were altered, some more than others, by my injury. My ears have suffered as a result of my fall, and I'm not really sure what the connection is with that. I have developed a condition called Diplacusis. That involves the inner ear. I'll try to explain.

In a healthy hearing process, each ear receives a sound and transmits it to the brain. Both signals are identical. When you have Diplacusis, the signals don't quite match. One ear is telling you one thing and the other is saying something slightly different.

That wasn't quite the way it manifested in my hearing, at least not in practice. I first became aware of it when I was listening to myself singing on one of my hit songs on a CD, from a record I had made years before. My singing sounded out of tune, even though I knew beyond any doubt I had done it right. My first thought was that maybe CDs start to degrade in quality at some point, but I soon found out that wasn't what was happening. I was able to adjust myself after a time, and it didn't affect my singing since that was an internally generated sound.

Even more unexpectedly, my ability to sing has been through its own changes. At first I wouldn't acknowledge the fact that anything was wrong with my singing voice except being out of shape, but I was wrong. When I finally got around to trying to put it back into shape (2010), I had a larynx specialist take scope photographs of my throat and he found that I had asymmetry in my vocal cords.

If this sounds mysterious, don't be alarmed. They had to explain it to me, too. Not only by what they meant by asymmetry, but what it had to do with my injury. It's because all of the muscles in the body work on a brain command, muscle response system. Most muscles perform one specific function, but the vocal cords, which are primarily a muscle, have to react to all sorts of different things like producing the different vowel sounds, all the different pitches, and a variety of other jobs. Things like growling, whining, falsetto tones and such, as well as many more mundane sounds. Therefore, when you have nerve damage to the brain, your cords start getting mixed commands, and often get out of alignment. Just to keep things accurate, many of those functions, and the formation of different sounds, like vowels, "consonant clusters" and such, are also the result of the work your tongue and lips do, but I'm trying to keep it simple here.

I eventually had to go on a specialized program of exercises to restore my cords to symmetry, but that's another story, and it didn't happen until much later.

Long before I found out about the wide-ranging effects my injury had caused in my body, something else took place. It happened in April of 2008, and it was totally unexpected. I guess it's wasn't that big a deal in the overall scheme of things, but it was important to me. It brought home the changes my life was going through and how much I subconsciously missed playing my music. Now that I had been sober for a while, those deep down urges were slowly worming their way back to the surface.

Here's what happened.

For several years, Jock Bartley had been trying to put the original Firefall band back together for a reunion concert. That spring, he was able to make the idea a reality. If it went well, perhaps the band could do a short tour.

It turned out to be a cross between a reunion and a merger of the original guys and the current band. There would be a live CD, and they were filming things in hopes of a possible DVD. There was no way to get the complete original band together because Michael Clarke had passed away. There had also been the question of whether I would be involved, initially because of my drinking, but more recently because of my injury. The fact that I hadn't been actively singing during the last several years also made my voice a valid concern.

In concert, the new version of the band played almost exclusively the old songs, so it would present no problem for Sandy Ficca, the current drummer, to fill Michael's spot. With me, it was slightly more complicated because of the same things. They intended to play all the old songs, most of which were mine. Since I was mobile now and able to get around, the main issue was my voice. Jock wasn't sure whether I could cut it, and to be honest, neither was I.

We all decided I would attend a rehearsal, give it a shot, and see how it sounded. There was a certain amount of disagreement within the band as far as who should decide whether I was doing an acceptable job. Some of the guys thought it should be my decision, whereas others thought Jock should make the call.

It was a moot point; both Jock and I agreed after I tried to sing "Just Remember I Love You" that it would not be in anyone's best interest for me to perform.

This was before I knew about the asymmetry in my vocal cords. I just didn't think I was doing the song justice after going so long without singing, and I didn't feel like I'd be doing my reputation any favors by trying to force it. I was also compelled to at least consider that my injury might have somehow had an effect on my voice.

When it came around to the night of the show, I chose instead just to attend. I was introduced and managed to walk up on stage on one crutch (I was showing off) where I spoke briefly about what a special event this was, and that I was sorry my health prevented me from participating. The audience gave me a very warm reception both when I went up and again after I spoke. During the course of the evening, I was flattered outrageously by numerous people who insisted it would never be the "real" Firefall unless I was involved.

Actually, I turned out to be the lucky one, because in the end the whole thing turned into a legal nightmare, with the rest of the original band and Jock so alienated from one another that even now they still haven't been able to work out their differences enough to agree on a contract, either for the live album or a DVD. Jock did go ahead and release a limited run of a CD, but as of this writing, any possibility of a DVD release is still unlikely. There has been some amount of reconciliation though, because David Muse and Mark Andes are back with the band again.

Once I realized my injury had had an effect on my singing voice, it was not much of a stretch to recognize that my speech had been affected as well. One of the byproducts of haunting the gym and being around people rather than sitting at home, was that I was involved in more conversations. And it soon became clear I needed a tune-up on my talker. Nothing major, but I had always spoken rather rapidly, and since my accident, my tongue was not quite up to the task of enunciating my thoughts as quickly as my mind was formulating them.

Since I had spoken at a fairly high rate of speed all my life, slowing it down was not an overnight adjustment. I tried my best to keep it to a more relaxed tempo, but the minute I got the least bit interested in a conversation, or a little excited, the rate went right back up there. Thus began another element in my recovery.

I began doing speech therapy with Ann Galloway at Longmont United Hospital in the middle of 2008. We went through a couple of preliminary sessions during which she simply listened to me talk and made notes about where she heard my weak points. She concentrated on words and sounds I slurred or slid over, as well as certain combinations of sounds that I seemed to have difficulty with. My sessions with her were once a week, but once she started putting me through my paces, she also gave me an extensive set of speech exercises to do at home.

Before too long, I found I was devoting more time on my own to these exercises than I was to my physical activities in the gym. Every day I spent nearly two hours doing word combinations, holding out a series of tones on the various different sounds (singing ah-a-e-o-eww on the notes G-A-B-C-D), and reading prepared exercises that had been designed to test my fluidity of tongue and speech. Alliteration was one end of the spectrum, with especially tricky changes of two connected words in the middle, and my favorite, sets of difficult "consonant clusters" at the other end. Those clusters consist of certain combinations of letters which, when bunched together, are tough to enunciate clearly in the course of speaking. And just for fun, try saying that last sentence five times as fast as you can!

I know I'm going into a lot of detail about this, but I'm hoping to convey the same feelings that I had while I was living it. It was all an endless flow of tiny little adjustments on the way to getting my mind and body fixed.

When I looked at it in pieces, it seemed like nothing of consequence was taking place in either my speech or my physical therapy, but when I stood back and tried to see the big picture, it all fell into place. What the therapists were getting me to do was (re)build a structure, which was me, one brick at a time.

As we got further along with the speech therapy, Ann told me I was making good progress, even though she worried that she was asking me to do too much in the way of homework. With each session, she would give me new exercises, but her conception of what I was supposed to do was different from mine. She wanted me to address only the new exercises and retire the others, whereas what I chose to do was simply add the new ones and continue to do all the ones she had given me previously. Before long, it was taking me nearly three hours a day to do the main body of work, and there were two or three of them that required a second go-round later in the evening. I didn't mind at all, but Ann kept apologizing to me. I tried to tell her I've always believed that anything worth doing is worth *over*doing. And I had my former lifestyle to prove it.

You Learn Somethin' New Every Day

By the beginning of 2009, I was deeply involved with both my speech therapy and my ongoing physical therapy. Between the two, I was staying busy, and I felt like I was beginning to see the results of the work I'd put in.

I was finally down to using one crutch in my everyday life. I was also doing most of my exercises without any supporting equipment, and beginning to take part in real-life activities again. I'd been off the bottle since Thanksgiving of 2007, and my mind was getting progressively clearer as the months passed. I never would have believed it if someone would have told me before I stopped drinking that I would still be shaking off the effects a year and a half after I quit. Little did I know then, but I would still be clearing out the mud for quite a few years yet.

My legs were almost back to their pre-accident strength, and I was spending an ever-increasing amount of my time in the gym concentrating on balance issues. Another thing that had surfaced during all this reconstructive work was that my fall in 2006 might not have originated my injury.

Subsequent checks on my EEGs indicated that my brain may have suffered some initial damage at an earlier time—most likely a number of years before my 2006 injury. The only possible culprit had to have been my car accident in 1987 when I shattered the windshield of my BMW with my forehead and took all those stitches in my face. When the subject came up with the neurologist about where my EEGs from that accident might be, I realized that none had ever been taken. He asked me to tell him about the event and whether I had noticed any significant body changes in the years following that crash.

As I described to him the circumstances of that night, how we went directly from the scene of the accident to the doctor's clinic, I started to piece together the facts relating to my physical condition and any changes I might have noticed. One obvious thing occurred to me almost immediately, and that was exactly when it was that I had first noticed I couldn't run.

I said in an earlier chapter that it was during my physical therapy that I realized that loss, but the fact is, I was only reminded of something that had *actually* come to my attention quite a while before that.

About four years prior to my fall, I found out that I had lost the ability to do anything more than walk. Of course, I hadn't had much occasion to be running, so I attributed the change to being out of shape, drinking, and the normal (albeit somewhat creepy) advance of my years.

But when I thought about it, I remembered it had only been a few months before I noticed my loss that I'd sprinted down a whole city block in pursuit of a car that was driving away. I caught the car, but I'm not trying to claim superhuman speed, because we were right in the middle of downtown Boulder, and I got a big assist from a red light. Nonetheless, I was running full speed and doing just fine. Then one day I attempted to break into a jog, and my body couldn't seem to get all the proper pieces going in sync.

As far as working with Helmut, I was now seeing him only every other week but I continued to do my workouts at least two or three times a week. That was when I added the jogging exercise up and down the hall eight times per workout. The hall was only twenty yards long, but when I was able to complete my circuits successfully, I felt the same sense of accomplishment as if I'd just run a marathon. The thrill of victory.

I tend to describe this whole series of events rather light-heartedly. The truth is, I definitely felt very frustrated at times when my body just wouldn't obey me, or do simple things I tried to make it do. But I also kept my sense of humor intact throughout the whole process. There was a reason for that. I believe, and my neurologists agree, that with brain injuries, more so than any other physical problem, a good and positive attitude is essential. It's simply a question of being unwilling to take no for an answer.

I'm not saying that you can do or cure anything simply because you believe you can. It doesn't work that way. I'm just saying that your chances of recovery are dramatically decreased if you *don't* believe.

That was the most important thing I needed to concentrate on and continue to do. I had to keep believing my condition was only a temporary setback in the big picture and that I *could* and *would* beat it in the end. I think one of the major weapons at my command was the idea that it was up to me to go on the attack. I had to be the aggressor. I knew it wouldn't be enough to do all the assigned exercises and follow the regular procedures if I really intended to get completely better. I had fought my way back from a wheelchair to a single crutch, though I knew the fight was far from over. I still had a long way to go.

One thing I've noticed and kind of touched on several times is the difficulty of holding on to hope. I've talked about the impermanence of mastering some skill only to find sometime later that it was out of my reach again. With all the forward and backward motion involved in recovery, all the progress I thought I'd made only to lose again, it would have been very easy to completely lose any hope that things would ever get back to normal.

And that can be the most powerful enemy anyone ever has to face.

You always have to remember that when you regress a step or two, you haven't lost anything more than a skirmish. Three steps forward, two steps back.

I use the word skirmish on purpose, because the whole thing has to be viewed as fighting a war. In a war, you have to realize that just because you gain ground doesn't mean you'll be able to hold on to it. More importantly, you have to believe that anything that's lost can be regained again. That's the way it went throughout my whole recovery experience.

I suppose this would be the point in time when I might conveniently say I just turned it over to God. In recent years, my pastor and good friend, Richie Furay, has told me what a wonderful testimony I could offer to people by explaining how I turned myself and my situation over to Him. I'm not really sure I can do that in total honesty. I never had any sort of epiphany or sudden moment of blinding awakening during my recovery. I am a firm believer in God, but I also subscribe to the adage that "God helps those who help themselves." I didn't feel like I could just sit back and wait for divine intervention to give me back the use of my legs, or settle my balance issues. I think faith is a valuable asset in recovery, but if you plan to salvage your situation, there is going to be a lot of flat-out hard work involved to implement the help you need from on high.

What I have come to realize was that my faith is a little different, but faith nonetheless. I can see now that even though it was never in my conscious perception of my predicament, I was still counting on God and His mercy. I had this quiet confidence that if I really gave it my very best effort, God wouldn't leave me in the situation I was in. And I wasn't even thinking that at the time. It was more a subconscious thing that I figured out way after the fact. It's not that I wasn't aware of the concept of "giving it to God," but I figured it wasn't going to get done if I just sat back and expected the Lord to heal me. My feeling has always been that God can open the door, but I'm the one who has to walk through it. To put it another way, He can make it possible, but it won't happen unless I do the footwork.

And another essential element a little closer at hand are the people who love you and continually inspire you and encourage you to keep at it, even when your own hopes are beginning to desert you. For me, it was Mary. She never left my side. There's another old saying that bears on this. "God works in mysterious ways." When I ask myself where Mary found the courage to fight my fight along with me for so long, it *is* a mystery. Perhaps God's hand was at work here.

Keepin' On, Keepin' On

Chapter Twenty

By the middle of 2009, I was making significant progress with the strength in my legs and my overall coordination. I began to think I was getting close to the point of finally saying goodbye to my single crutch once and for all. I had made the switch from a pair of crutches to a single crutch a while back and I felt like I was about due to take another step (pun not embraced, but unavoidable) forward. Originally, my plan had been to spend a couple of months on just the one, and then either go to a cane or maybe even start to walk free. It had always been my intention to move through each stage of recovery as quickly as possible. So I tended to be a little ambitious in my predictions about what I could and would do.

Unfortunately, I soon found out I was being way too optimistic about my progress, and ended up needing my crutch for quite a while longer than a couple of months. But I can't say the extension of time was a crushing blow. The fact is, when it came right down to it I was in less of a hurry to ditch the crutch than I thought I would be. Even the double crutches I used before that weren't so bad. But the walker? That was the one I hated. I had worked hard to put that device entirely into the past, because I never felt comfortable using one of them in the first place, no matter what the reason. A walker gave me the feeling that I was old, as well as disabled. That was very discouraging, because it made me feel like I had twice as many obstacles to overcome. So, naturally, I wanted to get done with that baby as soon as possible. On the other hand, my crutches were kind of neat. I had the kind that clasped around my forearm with a handle for my hand to grip. And in a way, they were sort of a security blanket and made me feel safe.

I was still seeing Helmut twice a month, and continuing to do a lot of independent work. I had my exercise regimen clearly established, and I was in the hospital workout area every other day or so. I usually spent an hour and a half doing my routine, and I got to be a very familiar face in the gym.

So I was still grinding through my workouts at least three times a week, and the advances I made were getting more dependable as far as holding true. My regressions were happening less often and were seemingly not as drastic in nature. Mary had Tuesdays and Fridays off, so we always hit the gym on those days. My sessions with Helmut were on Tuesdays, so Mary was there for them, and then helped me herself on Fridays.

When I was working with Helmut, Mary always kept a close eye on what we were doing so she could learn what exercises he was adding to my agenda, and then use the knowledge to help guide my regimen when he wasn't there. It all fell into a comfortable rhythm after a while, and I made slow but steady progress. When I say comfortable, I don't mean I was comfortable with my situation, but that it was a very regular and well-defined routine.

And while I say my progress was slow, that's only my opinion. The hospital personnel and the other regulars at the gym told me I was improving at an amazing rate of speed. However, to me, I was moving at a snail's pace.

One of the most important things I learned to do in order to keep up my enthusiasm and to stop myself from losing my drive was to make myself look back not at yesterday or last week, but to compare where I was right then with where I had been a couple of months back. That also helped me to react less to the two steps forward, one step back aspect of my circumstances.

I think it was also my first experience with having to give more than lip service to the idea of patience. Patience was a concept I had never mastered.

I also finally got a handle on what people mean when they say, "It's a process, not an event."

I tried to broaden the range of exercises that Helmut laid out for me. Adlibbing comes naturally to me, and I couldn't imagine a more suitable place to use that ability than trying to compliment my program.

One thing I did was try to come up with little things I could do almost anywhere to sharpen my brain-muscle coordination. With brain injuries, a lot of the trick was reprogramming the circuits in my head into unused and undamaged areas.

For instance, I would do things like placing my hand flat on a table and then lift my fingers one at a time in a sequence of ongoing variations. For example, 1-2-3-4, 1-3-2-4, 1-4-2-3, 4-3-2-1. I'd do that about five times, and then change up my sequencing. There are practically an unending number of different combinations to pick from, as long as I could keep from letting it become automatic. I just had to make sure each command came right off the top of my head.

I did something similar when I had to sit and wait somewhere. I'd do a little tapping routine. One toe, one heel, one toe, two heel, two toe, one heel, two toe, three heel, or any combination of numbers as long as I kept changing them up. The whole idea was to make my body interpret and react to the message my brain was sending, even as it altered. And to never let a steady pattern develop. The most important element of what I was trying to do was to keep everything random so that I couldn't start to perform the routines by using muscle memory.

I've always liked the concept of reaching into those untapped areas of the mind anyway. I'm told humans only use about 15% of our brain, and some people who know about such things believe it to be an even smaller percentage. One way or the other, that leaves a whole lot of space to work with on expansion. If I work hard, who can say where it might lead. Who knows? Maybe one day, I'll be able to move furniture with nothing but the power of my mind. That strikes me as a much more practical use of telekinesis than bending spoons.

* * *

Just in case I might have stopped paying attention during those years while I was working on my recovery, my body decided I should have a few additional surprises. I discovered I had cataracts, which I had to have surgically repaired, not to mention that one day while I was just sitting at home, watching TV and not really bothering anybody, the dental bridge fell out of my mouth. I guess that's another thing that requires a little explanation.

Back in 1999, Mary and I were living in Boulder, still in the same place we had been since she moved in with me after I came back from California. Our house was set back off the street, and one of my designated "husband chores" was taking out the trash. Being responsible citizens, we always separated our regular garbage from our recyclables.

At that time, we were putting our old newspapers in a big wooden orange crate, and on collection day I would carry it out to the curb along with the other cans. The only thing was that when I was carrying the recycling out, I couldn't see the ground directly in front of me. From the house to the street was a long walkway paved with flagstones. (Ah yes, the infamous flagstones again. Actually, this was the first time they ambushed me.) The problem was that each individual stone protruded a little bit above the ground, just enough to catch the unwary. Since I couldn't see where I was going, I caught my toe on one, and when I fell I took one of the corners of the orange crate directly on my right eyetooth. The tooth broke off quite nicely just above my gums.

I started to bleed profusely, and when I went back inside I told Mary that I thought maybe we should call the dentist. We did, and then drove immediately over to his office where he removed the stump of my tooth and began the process of designing me a bridge. To make a long story short, I had that bridge until the quiet afternoon years later, when it decided to terminate its residency in my mouth. Even though that happened shortly after I lost my ability to walk, it wasn't until I started my therapy months later that I discovered how ghastly I looked. I bore a striking resemblance to a new-age vampire, and if I had been a child on the receiving end of a smile from someone who looked like I did, I would have run screaming to my mother in fright!

The thing is, when you're either crawling around your house, or rolling around in a wheelchair, you don't get many opportunities, nor are you very interested in looking in any mirrors. Especially at my own ugly mug.

When You Feel Like Cryin', But...

But let's get back to my recovery and some of the more peripheral elements of it. I've already mentioned that during the time shortly after my injury I started to borrow against my royalties. I also said I didn't much care at the time. It didn't seem to be that big a deal. Besides, I didn't really have much choice in the matter. There were bills to pay, and my main source of income for a number of years had been my royalties. In the normal course of events, the amount of money coming in took care of the outlay, but once there were additional medical expenses it tipped the scales and destroyed the balance.

Everybody knows the cost of routine medical care these days is off the charts, and if you're not insured when something major happens, you can find yourself broke and piling up serious debts before you know what hit you. My own ability to acquire insurance had pretty much disappeared when they discovered the blood clots in my leg and when I went through my seizure period. I became a poster boy for the old "pre-existing condition" runaround. The only chance I had for any coverage at all was as a dependent on Mary's work policies, and that had been on and off because she had changed jobs several times.

Well before I hit the hospital at Thanksgiving of 2007, we were facing a serious cash crunch due to the cost of the early stages of therapy and the visits to my neurologist. With the addition of the hospital episode, borrowing was the only option. I ended up spending over a week in the ICU, and from there on, royalty loans became an ongoing cycle. Even when I had coverage as a dependent of Mary's work insurance, it didn't cover the areas I needed. I'm talking about voice coaching and hypnotherapy sessions. And I haven't even told you about those things yet.

I bring all that up just to initiate describing my state of mind at that point. I've said I managed to keep a positive attitude about my situation and was determined not to let my condition be a permanent one. That's true, but it doesn't mean that I didn't spend more than a few nights either unable to sleep or having some very disturbing dreams when I *did* manage to drift off.

No matter how positive my attitude was, it was pretty hard not to have questions about whether I was fooling myself about making a full recovery. I told myself I was making progress. When I looked at the longer view I knew I was, but the hard fact remained that there were many things I simply couldn't do no matter how hard I tried.

Lame Brain

Fighting the feeling of overall helplessness was a full-time job. I have to admit it's not that easy to remember exactly how I was feeling in those days, and I'm pretty sure it's mostly a matter of my mind choosing to stash those memories deep inside my head. I can recollect the overall emotions, but it takes a conscious effort, and it's not something I particularly enjoy doing.

But there were other, more positive lessons to be learned. Among the things I realized was that even when things seem to be totally beyond your reach, you have to persevere. No battle is truly lost until you surrender, and *every* battle is lost when you do (surrender, that is). And sometimes just when you least expect it, things can turn for the better. My feeling is there are far fewer situations than we think which truly qualify as lost causes.

I am certain that a good attitude is a major factor in recovering from a brain injury. But that's not the only place where a positive attitude is a crucial ally. I think the same concept applies to almost any health issue, and quite a number of other things to boot. As the saying goes "You gotta' believe." I don't think belief alone will turn the trick, but if you *don't* believe, you've reduced your chances of success. And besides, that's only half the equation. I think that in most cases, if you *do* believe, you will markedly *improve* your chances of beating the situation. Almost any situation. So it's not just a definite loss when you don't, it's a definite gain when you do (believe, that is). It comes under the heading of confidence.

There's another aspect of recovery that can't be ignored, and that's how tiring it is. I'm not talking about the physical demands, although there's no question that they can be taxing. I'm talking about how emotionally and mentally exhausting it can be. Your physical condition becomes the primary factor in every decision you make from the most important to the most mundane. It's not only whether you can comfortably attend some major event, but how much you want that glass of water or how badly you have to go to the bathroom. The ever-present nature of having to weigh everything against whether you can do it easily or whether in fact you can do it *at all* tends to eventually wear away your resolve. Believe me, that can be a major contributor to the attitude you bring to your effort to get your life back together.

That makes the emotional fatigue element another of the major unseen enemies to recovery. And it may be the hardest one to defeat. It seems incredibly ironic to consider that while a person is focused on beating their disability, and getting closer and closer to winning that battle, they end up getting done in by the little day-to-day harassments that accompany the fight. And the most disturbing thing is…you can never quite put your finger on what it is you're fighting. As soon as you come face-to-face with your disability and can identify what you're up against, you can take that struggle directly to the problem. But before then, the little stuff nags at you without really taking any firm shape.

Once again, it's very much like being in a war. The disability is the army you're fighting against right out there in the open facing you on the field of battle. You know what you have to do to attack and hopefully defeat it. But those other things that you don't pay much attention to are like guerillas that slip in under the radar, and hit and run. They hide behind the scenes and poke you when you're not looking. And there are no fixed battles. They're always lingering on the edges of the situation, ready to chip away at your confidence and impede your progress. Before you know it, you'll find all your hopes for recovery starting to fade into the shadows.

And that's exactly the time when you need them most of all.

You Put Your Right Foot In…

Chapter Twenty-One

Let's get back to 2009—because some important things were happening then, too. More accurately, some things that were significant.

In early August, after depending on it for what seemed like a lifetime, I finally put down my last crutch. Even though it had served me well, first for support and later in the role of a security blanket, it was wonderful to finally be moving around free of any walking aids for the first time in over three years.

My 60th birthday was coming up at the end of the month, and I think that subconsciously, I had already made up my mind to be crutch-free as a present to myself by that date. It didn't really hit me until later how remarkably fortunate I was to get the full use of my legs back at all, much less on any kind of set time schedule. I owe a great debt of gratitude to Mary and Helmut for encouraging me to keep plugging away, even when the process seemed to be taking an eternity.

My old musical pal, Chris Hillman, once told me that he thought God had a specific plan in mind for me, which makes sense, since I'm pretty sure God has a plan in mind for each of us. Nonetheless, I don't think I could ask for much clearer evidence than my recovery. And that's in spite of the fact that I'm still not quite sure exactly what that plan might be. All I can say is that I feel incredibly blessed.

A year earlier I had had a conversation with another dear friend of mine who is an actress in Los Angeles. She's a few years older than I am and she had called to wish me a happy birthday. When she asked me how old I was going to be and I said fifty-nine, she told me she was delighted for me. When I asked her why, she said it was because I could look forward to ten very exciting years before I turned sixty.

Since she was an actress, that made perfect sense, at least if you used Hollywood math. As it turned out, she was partially right. It did feel like ten years between the time I turned fifty-nine and the time I turned sixty. But only because my recovery seemed to be taking so long.

Now it was August 31st again and I was about to celebrate my sixtieth birthday. On that day something else happened which had quite an impact on me.

Mary and I went up to Copper Mountain ski resort to see a music festival, featuring all country rock bands. Chris Hillman and the Desert Rose Band, Poco, The Nitty Gritty Dirt Band, Pure Prairie League, and Firefall (the current version) were all playing.

As I mingled with some of the guys backstage, I realized that I counted at least one member of every act as a friend. And when I watched them do their shows, I was once again reminded how much I missed being up there myself. What hit me hardest was the realization that no matter what my own perception of myself was, in reality, I was no longer the new kid on the block, and if I ever intended to do any more musical work, I needed to get moving. That was the day I made up my mind to get re-involved with my music on a professional basis.

I knew I couldn't expect to just pick things up from where I left off, as if my life hadn't changed. Not to mention that it was a different audience now, too. It had been years since I worked, and to say the least, and my chops were rusty. It was going to take some time to sharpen up my musical skills, if in fact I could do it at all. But I did have a number of unreleased songs I had recorded before I hurt my hand and head, so at least I knew I had *some means* of starting my reentry process.

Considering that my physical recovery from my head injury was now pretty much accomplished, I was ready for a new challenge, and I figured I had just found it. It was time to begin my new life.

But there was another challenge to deal with before I could even start thinking about my musical skills. If I wanted to get any more of my already recorded music out there, I had to decide how to go about doing it.

As I saw my potential options, I could look for a record label who specialized in "classic artists" (they also call them "archival artists," but that name makes me shudder), and turn what I considered to be the best of my unreleased material over to them and have them put out on a CD, or I could see about putting my stuff out there myself using the Internet.

But that was only the first step of a very complicated process I was going to have to learn to navigate. I hadn't been aware of just how much the whole music business had changed since I had stepped out of the loop. Deciding to jump back in was like stepping onto a moving train. I felt like the kid whose dad teaches him to swim by just throwing him into the deep end of the pool and telling him to start paddling.

I only had a passing awareness of things like iTunes because it didn't even exist when I was in the middle of my career. Now I knew the platforms were there, but I didn't have a clue about how to use them to merchandise my music.

When it came right down to it, since I hadn't been paying attention to the monumental changes in the music industry between the time I walked away from it and the present, I was going to need a crash course in almost every aspect of what was going on out there.

In making my decision about how to present my material, I had several things to consider.

First of all, I only had a finite number of songs on tape or disc, and there was no way of knowing how long it would be before I was ready to record anymore. With that as a consideration, I took a closer look at the attention span of audiences these days. There don't seem to be that many people who take the time or expend the energy to really listen to a whole album anymore. Certainly there are still some folks who pay complete attention when they listen, but not nearly as many as there used to be. Most people are just too busy or in too much of a hurry to spend that long on one thing.

As a result of that mindset, when a new CD comes out, many of the listeners concentrate on two or three songs, and the rest of the album falls through the cracks. Lately, I've seen evidence that more of the powers that be in music are taking that into consideration because there has been something of a revival of the EP—the four-song collections that some artists have begun to put out again.

Secondly, I didn't know if I would be best served by releasing my songs a few at a time, and if I did, whether I would still have the option of signing with a label. There was also the question of whether people who would be most likely to be my audience were the same ones who were getting their music online—or were my fans still exclusively buying CDs?

I spoke to a couple of people at the labels who had expressed an interest in my music, and generally, they were not too excited by the idea of releasing EP-sized collections.

I then explored the idea of putting out the EP collections on CDs myself. I found out that there are companies who do a thing called "short runs." That means that they will print your disc, EP or CD, in any quantity you want from one to a couple of thousand so you can gauge the response without taking the risk of pressing huge amounts before you know if anybody wants one.

Since I knew I needed an education, I started asking questions of the people I knew who would be most likely to have answers. The first folks I went to were my friends who were involved with record stores. From them, I got a surprising consensus. The question was really centered not so much on who bought what, but where they were buying it.

When I asked my questions, my friends almost all asked me the same rather unexpected question in return. They wanted to know if I was planning on touring to support the release of my music. They said that a very large chunk of the CDs being sold now were at the concert venues, and if I wasn't planning to tour, it probably wouldn't be cost effective to release a hard copy. Since I knew I wouldn't be doing any live performing any time soon, I took my friends' advice, and decided to simply release my songs online.

One thing I've mentioned only briefly is that up until shortly before that point in time I had refused to involve myself with computers for any reason at all. I know that makes me something of a dinosaur, but it's my opinion that with every step we take that lessens or removes actual personal contact, we isolate ourselves more as human beings. It's pretty common these days to hear about the disintegration of our ability to make simple human contact with other people, or to watch kids who choose to communicate exclusively by texting or Tweeting.

I had finally surrendered to technology for the purpose of getting in touch with old friends I'd lost track of and couldn't locate any other way. I opened a Facebook account.

And with my choice to use the net to get my music out there, I had to do a big reorganization of my attitudes. Even though I did, I'd still rather talk to somebody in person or on the phone when I have a choice.

Anyway, since I had made the decision to market my music by way of the net, I made my peace with my PC, but in truth it was only an uneasy truce. On the home front, Mary was still having problems with computer intrusion, which had magnified from an annoyance to a major disruption in our lives. I've already described the merry-go-round ride we experienced when we tried to get help from the proper authorities, so suffice it to say that jumping into the technological age made me more than a trifle nervous.

With only our ongoing problems to use as a frame of reference, you can probably understand why I pretty much entered the "circuit world" kicking and screaming. But since I had already relaxed my once-rigid dismissal of computers to find old friends, it was easier to compromise a second time. I also discovered I could make use of Facebook to promote the music I was putting out there. By simply alerting the people on my friend list, I could make them aware I had new stuff out there, whereas otherwise they might not have known.

That leads me to another area that I had to try to find a way to deal with, and more new information I had to absorb about the changed world of music. I had hoped that some residual name recognition might help me get a bit of initial FM radio airplay. Unfortunately, that was based on the false assumption that FM was still more free form and less regimented than AM. That was how it *used* to be. That's *not* how it is now. Most FM stations now have just as tightly programmed a playlist as AM ever did, and trying to break into it is nearly impossible without the support of a record label, a high-powered marketing organization, or a victory on "American Idol". And besides, no radio station goes searching for its music online. I would have had to actually make some CDs and get them out there.

From what I hear, upwards of 80% of the major-market FM stations buy their

Lame Brain

play lists from two or three programming suppliers, so everywhere you turn your dial, you're going to hear the same tunes.

I had none of the aforementioned supports, and I found my "name value" was worth zip in that area. I also became aware of a funny little quirk concerning radio. A natural black hole has formed in recent years on radio for artists like me. Here's how it works. The "classic radio" stations want to play music from established artists, but what they want is those artists' established music. The old hits. On the other hand, the stations that want to play new music want it from new artists. Therefore, new music from old artists has almost no place to call home. There are, luckily, a few exceptions that cater to new stuff from old guys. There is a syndicated Internet station called C.A.T (Classic Artists Today) that specializes in just such material. And there are also a few FM stations that refuse to buckle under the tight playlists that are the current order of the day. I probably shouldn't complain. A couple of my songs ("You Are the Woman" and "Just Remember") are on those lists, but it certainly makes it difficult to get something new into play.

I released my first collection in April of 2010. I chose to affiliate with Independent Online Distribution Alliance* (IODA). They were in the business of distributing material to the major vendors, like iTunes, Amazon, CD Baby, and most all the others. The difference between approaching things through them and going with one of the vendors directly was that you couldn't just sign up with IODA by paying a fee. You had to be accepted by them. They functioned very much like record labels used to, only they did it in the Internet world. They required not only your songs, but a virtual album cover, liner notes, credits, and pretty much everything you would include if you were releasing a hard copy CD.

That suited me fine, because in my own life I have always taken great pleasure in the whole record experience, which includes all of those things. When I was a teenager, my friends and I used to spend hours poring over the liner notes and perusing the credits to see who did what on each song. The covers were an art form of their own.

One of the harder elements of choosing not to release my songs in hard copy form was the reluctance to abandon all those extra delights. When I put out my first collection, I even had to come up with a name for it. I decided to call it *Phases*, because I was using music I had written and recorded over a long span of time, and in several different circumstances. When I put the collection out, I was lucky to have a few old DJ friends who premiered a song or two, and I made a couple of new friends who did the same. So I managed to garner a little airplay, but most of the entry doors were closed. Still, my songs found their way to a few longtime dedicated fans and I'm grateful for that. Those people gave me a reason to think that maybe if I stuck with it, I could still get my music out there.

*Subsequently bought by The Orchard Company.

Rosanne Rosannadana Was Right
(It's Always Something)
Chapter Twenty-Two

When I spoke about being diagnosed with asymmetry in my vocal cords, it may have sounded as if I decided to go see a larynx doctor on the odd chance I might need one. Even I'm not that crazy-paranoid.

The thing is, after I had figured out the details of how I wanted to get my music out there, the time had come to start sharpening my performance skills. The obvious place to start was with my voice.

I hadn't been singing actively for far too long, and since the voice is a muscle, I realized mine was completely out of shape. I asked a friend of mine who used to be a vocal coach (but had since retired), for a referral to someone else. His recommendation was a woman named Kate Emerich down in Denver. He said she was an operatic diva herself, and she had worked with a number of artists who were either recovering from injury or attempting to come back after a prolonged inaction (retirement).

When I managed to contact Kate, she would only see me on the condition that I first consult her associate, Dr. Opperman, who was, you guessed it, a larynx specialist. That's how I came to find out about the situation with my vocal cords.

After we had ascertained my condition, I started a series of sessions with Kate in the summer of 2010 and began strengthening my voice through a whole different set of exercises than the ones I had needed to improve my speech. There was some overlap, but not nearly as much as I expected. Among other things, Kate chose exercises that would work toward resynchronizing my rebellious cords.

Once again I found myself spending a large chunk of my time each day doing my vocal work. And once again, my method was to take each new exercise and simply add it to what I was already doing.

Before long, I was doing scales and sounds and some other highly improbable types of vocal gyrations for two or three hours at a time. I didn't have a problem with that, because little by little, I could hear my voice coming around. Kate told me early on that her normal course of treatment was six sessions, but she thought it would be a good idea to double that amount in my case.

When I say *improbable*, I'm not exaggerating. I won't go into all of them, but my favorite was the one where I was asked to puff out my cheeks and blow out the air while singing a descending line of boyde-boyde-boyde-boyde-bo. There were several other equally unlikely endeavors, but they all had a purpose, no matter how difficult for me to understand, and they seemed to be making a difference.

I was also encouraged, and flattered, when she told me that once my voice got back into shape, she'd like to sing with me sometime. Of course, she may have said that to all her patients, just to motivate them. But I admit somewhere inside I still felt a jolt of the old self confidence I used to have about my voice (that familiar "of course you would" cockiness).

As things worked out, I had done eight sessions with her when the insurance company informed us that they did not consider retraining my voice as essential therapy to my recovery so I had to discontinue the remainder of my appointments. Frankly, I can think of very few things more important to *my* recovery than being able to sing again. But I guess that's the insurance game.

I already had a substantial amount of exercises from the lessons I'd taken incorporated into my daily routine, so I wasn't left high and dry. I just kept on doing the same exercises, even the outrageous-sounding ones, and I could feel my vocal muscles slowly getting stronger.

The next thing I had to work on was my guitar playing. I put that off for quite a while. Even before my brain injury I had been having a very tough time trying to play as a result of cutting my hand and the subsequent ligament damage. As I have mentioned, my first problem had been an inability to hold onto a flat pick. I thought I might be able to solve that dilemma by thinking outside the box a little. I got together with an engineer friend of mine and came up with a concept. We designed a pick that allowed for the lack of strength in my finger and helped me hold on without losing it every time I back strummed. My friend and I haven't decided whether we want to make it available for public sale yet, but it sure made it easier for *me* to play.

At that point, I no longer had any excuse not to begin working on my playing. The minute I tried to strum, I found one. I was so clumsy I felt like I was wasting my time. It seemed clear to me that trying to learn how to play again with any semblance of skill was going to be beyond my reach. But there was something else I had gleaned from my vocal sessions with Kate. And even though it seemed like just a strange question at the time, it turned out to be pretty important. Without any buildup, she asked me one day if I ever rehearsed mentally. Since I didn't know what that meant, I said I probably hadn't.

It turned out that what she was talking about was visualizing myself singing like I did back in the days when I was doing it all the time. I told her that I had never tried that, but that I did have fairly frequent dreams in which I was singing as well as I ever had. Did that count?

Yes, she said, and was very excited. She went on to say I had given her much stronger evidence of what she was trying to establish—that the memories of doing it were still stored in my brain somewhere. And having dreams about it spontaneously was a far better sign of those memories being there than trying to consciously conjure up the experience. It was just a matter of reconnecting the circuitry after the damage I'd done.

Since in those dreams I was also playing guitar as well as I had in the old days, I thought the same principle might apply. I asked my neurologist about it and he said that it was indeed very similar, except that now we were talking about a sense (i.e. muscle) memory. That meant the proper nerve connections with the muscle had to be reestablished. I'm thinking maybe he didn't consider the vocal cords to be a muscle. To each his own.

I'm still waiting for the illusive reconnection day, but I've kept on practicing and I believe I'm making progress. Granted, it seems to be taking forever, but so did my experience in learning to walk again. So once again, I have to practice a little patience. And I've got a philosophy about it that keeps me working on things.

It goes something like this...

Way back when I was fifteen and first picked up a guitar, I used to play eight or ten hours a day to get better. Even so, it all seemed to fall into place without me giving it all that much effort. By my reckoning, it didn't seem like all that big a job. Maybe that's because at that age, everything is ahead of you. Anyway, with that in mind, if I have to work a bit harder to recover my abilities, it sort of balances things out.

I admit to feeling a little cosmically short-changed in one respect. I'm left-handed, and if I had hit the right side of my forehead, it would have been my left side that suffered the nerve-muscle impairment (because of the right brain-left side, left brain-right side hemisphere thing). That would have required me to do much more work to develop my right hand for simple everyday activities like handwriting and eating. Ideally, I might have ended up being ambidextrous. Actually, I'm only kidding about the ambidextrous thing, but rehabilitating my left side would probably have been a little easier due to a larger amount of sense memory. But fate, and all its caprices, were not through fooling around with me quite yet.

Just when I started getting serious about strumming every day, I broke my right wrist while doing one of my exercises in August of 2010. That postponed my guitar work for several months. Once again, notice it was my *right* wrist, not my left, so I was denied yet another chance to develop that side, and instead, just magnified my reliance on my left side. I'm even more left-handed now than I used to be.

* * *

I put out my second four-song collection in October of 2010, six months after the first one. I called it *Same Mirror, Different Reflections*. There was no deep hidden meaning in that title; it just seemed appropriate if I considered myself the mirror and the songs the reflections. Mainly, I just liked the sound of it.

I found myself in pretty much the same situation as I had been with *Phases*. A few of my friends on the more independent stations played a couple of the songs, but overall, I was still hitting a wall when it came to breaking through on the play lists of the major stations. And getting airplay on major stations was probably a pipe dream anyway. I had never been a superstar even at the height of my involvement with rock and roll. Firefall had a nice run for a while, and I had managed to write a number of popular songs that made the charts, but that had been quite a number of years ago. I had to face the fact that by this point in time, any fame I might once have laid claim to was nothing more than a rusty, old trophy by now.

Those independent stations were my lifeline, so I'll always be grateful to people like Ray White at C.A.T. and a station owner in North Carolina named Bill Benjamin (among others) for debuting songs from both the first and second collections on their stations. Both Bill's station, Magic 95.9, and C.A.T. are Internet operations, so they're available everywhere. Having my songs on these outlets allowed people who might otherwise not have known I was active again to hear the new songs.

Other than that, it was a long term slow-growth situation. Things were quietly changing behind the scenes, but not very quickly. I was making more friends who were involved in music as time went by, largely as a result of the Internet and Facebook. Some of them were in radio which helped, and bit by bit, my music was getting heard and being played for more people a few plays at a time.

I'm not talking about any major impact, because the number of stations was still so small I could pretty much count them on my fingers, but any progress was enough to give me hope that at some point the right person would take notice and carry one of my songs to a much larger audience. And maybe, just maybe make my pipe dream come true.

When I use terms like "pipe dreams", it makes it sound like my goals were something other than what they actually were. I wasn't hoping to suddenly become a big star as a result of putting music out again. I chased that dream for a long time when I was on the first go-round. No, at this point what I was hoping for was to have my music heard again and use that as a basis to being able to get out and work some on my own terms. I wasn't yet thinking of putting another band together or doing any serious touring.

Particularly touring. That specific animal is a young man's game. Even when I *was* a young man, going on the road for two or three weeks at a time was an exhausting way to make a living. So I was looking for something a little more like reality than the whirlwind I had once known all too well.

Once again, I found a perfect work model in the approach taken by my old friend, Chris Hillman. Like me, Chris too had decided that he had seen enough of the tour circuit, but he still loved music and wanted to play. What he chose to do was team up with Herb Pedersen and go out as a duo every couple of weeks or so and play a weekend somewhere. That eliminated carrying all that equipment around to stage a big production and left him free to pursue a real life most of the time. Also, it kept the overhead down so that he could still generate a little money from it.

That's a plus, because I'm not against making a living, either. I also knew that all those plans were dependent on me getting back into playing and singing shape, so at that juncture, it was still a moot point. But when the time came that I felt ready to try, I thought maybe an acoustic act would be the path to go.

So, when I healed from my broken wrist, I had to discipline myself to stay consistent about practicing. It was hard to maintain any enthusiasm when I didn't seem to be making any progress, but as I said, I knew it was going to take some honest-to-goodness work, and besides, there was always the potential that any day might be "reconnection day." My voice was improving faster than my playing, so that motivated me a little, and an even bigger motivation was that for all the years since I originally cut my hand and had to quit playing, my mind had been continuing to store up all those lyric ideas for songs as yet unwritten. That meant if I could even improve to the point of being able to block out some basic rhythms and chord progressions, I could start lightening my backlog of song ideas and get back to composing again.

As I did my daily guitar work, I made a few changes to help the process along. For the first time in my life, I abandoned medium gauge strings in favor of light gauge, and I tried out a light gauge flat pick instead of my usual medium gauge model. I had gained enough strength in my index finger to make the custom model unnecessary for me, especially with the added flexibility of the light gauge pick. Since I could now use a regular pick again, I abandoned my custom model. I thought the process of making enough of them to keep me supplied might get a bit too expensive.

From that point on, I have found the hardest thing to overcome as far as sticking with my practice routine is fear. The fear that no matter how hard I try, the damage has been done. The fear I won't ever be able to play well enough to sit in with old friends, or just pick up a guitar and play in front of anybody. I suppose a lot of that comes from ego and pride based on what I used to be able to do. But whatever the source, that's the way it is, and I can't make believe I don't feel that way.

It's hard to go on believing I'll get my chops back when the process moves so very slowly. I have to keep reminding myself of all the things I discovered about being patient and not abandoning goals when I was learning to walk again.

Once More With Feeling

Changing my choice of strings and picks was not the only thing I tried to facilitate my guitar playing. My brain injury had taught me a lot about patience, but impatience can be a persistent character trait, and a difficult one to eradicate. I found it very frustrating to be unable to do simple things that I had done so naturally and easily on my instrument in the forty years I've been playing. I was willing to try some unorthodox methods in hopes of making some sort of breakthrough.

Since my neurologist had agreed that my dreams indicated I still retained the sense memory of how to play like I did before my injury, I went looking for ways to open that door in my mind. It occurred to me to try hypnotherapy. (Quite honestly, it still seems like an idea that ought to work. The whole idea of hypnosis is to get into your subconscious mind, and with the help of the therapist, bring whatever necessary information is catalogued there back up to the surface.) I was lucky enough to find a highly qualified and very sympathetic hypnotherapist right in Longmont by the name of Zoilita Grant.

Zoilita came with the best references and recommendations from numerous others in her field, and she had served as president of the Colorado Association of Psychotherapists for four and a half years between January, 2004 and May, 2008.

I worked with Zoilita for about three months on a weekly basis, but the costs were directly out of pocket because once again, the insurance people did not consider the treatment as essential to my recovery. I guess I can see how they might see it that way because from an insurer's point of view, even psychiatry, not to mention hypnotism, is suspect as medical treatment. I think some of those insurance guys also belong to the Flat Earth Society; or maybe I just didn't have the right coverage.

I can't say what my treatment would have led to since I couldn't afford to continue it long enough to find out. We were still exploring various methods of finding the right buttons to push to pull out the information we were looking for. There's a whole lot of stuff in the brain, and chances are, my brain has more "stuff" than most. It seems like people have been telling me I was full of "stuff" all my life.

Long after I discontinued my hypnotherapy experiment I kept on plugging away at the more mundane approach to getting better by practicing my strumming and doing my vocal exercises. As I said, my voice was coming back faster than my guitar chops, but both were slowly (albiet, *very* slowly) gaining ground, and by early 2011, I had reached the point where I could block out my chords and do a basic strum and sing rough versions of some of my old songs. I had also started to use what tools I could muster to start composing again. I still hadn't tumbled to the fact that I could compose without my instrument, so everything took a lot longer.

About that time I was confronted with something I hadn't seen coming. It had been almost a year and a half since I pronounced myself fully recovered from my brain injury. I had been working diligently to gain enough pick control to start making some serious inroads into playing passable guitar again. I suppose I was so busy concentrating on the managing of my pick that I overlooked a much more fundamental issue. I still had one lingering consequence from my brain damage. The problem was my right arm. Even though I was able to do the basic up and down rhythmic strum, when I tried anything more complex or sophisticated, my arm wouldn't do what I was asking it to do. The natural working order of things is brain command, muscle response. In my body, the sequence went more like this:

Brain: "Do a double down stroke, then a quick up strum."

Arm: "You talkin' to me, sucker?"

No connection and no cooperation. It was neither graceful nor accurate. In fact, what it was, was very, very discouraging.

So as you might imagine, the first two new additions to my composing catalogue were somewhat limited musically by what I couldn't do, but I managed to write things that were suited to my abilities, and they seemed to work as songs.

I also decided it was about time to test the waters vocally. I began to go out to some of the little local places occasionally, and sit in on a song or two with some of my friends. I initially just sang a little harmony, which was the safest thing to do. You can sort of hide behind the lead vocalist when you sing harmony. All you have to get right is your pitch. It doesn't require the quality of tone that you need when your voice is out there in front of everyone else's. When you do that, you're pretty much vocally naked.

That experiment went pretty well, and in July of 2011, I was feeling confident enough to sit in with Firefall in front of an audience of a couple of thousand people. I was still just singing harmonies of course, but it was another step in the right direction. To my great relief, that appearance went off well, too. Or at least I thought it did. The audience seemed to enjoy it and the comments people made to me were very complimentary and led me to believe things were coming right along. I have since been told by at least one of my old band mates that

I wasn't very good. I'm still holding out hope that he was wrong, but I *have* started a new course of vocal lessons to help me make the most of my voice. I don't mean to say that my voice will be as good as it ever was because even now I'm still working to improve it; and I'm a whole lot older than I was in the prime of my career. But I am hoping my singing will not be as lacking as the picture my bandmate painted for me.

During that same span of time, I had put together another four-song collection and called it *Full Bloom*. It was supposed to be posted online by summer, but there were some delays with the artwork and there was one song I decided to replace and save for a later set because I realized I wanted to add some harmony behind the lead vocal. As a result, the final version of *Full Bloom* wasn't released until November of 2011. I intended to put out two or three more collections, but there have been some changes in that situation. Now I think I might wait and re-record the songs I've already got out there, and only release fresh versions of the other stuff that's not out there yet. If that sounds like I have a new musical vehicle, I do.

I've continued to gain confidence after my first halting steps into the performance arena, and progressed to sing some lead vocals again. I went into the studio and cut two lead vocals and three harmony parts in four hours for an album that some friends from Italy were doing. During the middle of the taping I realized it was my first recording session in over twenty years! Later, I sang two songs at a benefit and someone in the audience put the performance on YouTube. And finally, I went to Florida and did a whole set of my best known songs, backed by a complete band of session players and came away feeling like I was ready to start working again. That all happened in the middle part of 2012.

And something very interesting happened towards the end of 2012. David Muse contacted all of the original members of Firefall, plus Bobby Caldwell to play drums, Paul Cotton from Poco as a second lead guitarist, and two or three other hot-shot players from Florida. Plus, Joe Lala, who was the unofficial seventh member of Firefall, was invited to play percussion. Everyone but Larry Burnett said yes, and he had to decline due to concerns about his own health needs. Being diabetic, he had a huge monthly expense to cover his insulin and such, and he would have had to sacrifice the health insurance his current job was providing. It wasn't a Firefall reunion anyway, but an entirely different thing. The idea was for everyone involved to bring something from their own musical associations to the table, and then we could pick what we wanted to construct a review-type show from out of all that we had available.

After a rehearsal or two, Paul Cotton decided there were a few too many guitar players and dropped out as well. With the people still involved, we were able to choose from things the members had been personally involved with from Spirit, JoJo Gunne, Heart, Dan Fogelberg (Mark), The Byrds, The Flying

Burrito Brothers, Stephen Stills, Linda Rondstadt (me), Zephyr, Gram Parsons and the Fallen Angels (Jock), Marshall Tucker (David), and even Canned Heat (Mark was their first bass player). And that's just from the guys from Firefall and only the credits we had with name bands. Remember, the concept was for all of us to bring whatever we had and wanted to share.

Then we added Johnny Winter, Rick Derringer, and Captain Beyond (Bobby). Joe Lala had a catalogue of credits too long to list. Suffice it to say that Joe was an original member of Blues Image, and if we wanted to include anything from The Bee Gees or CSN or more others than I can count, Joe also had the resume to justify that. In the end, we chose to do a little bit of everything.

It was a fun project, but it didn't last very long. The people involved lived in different parts of the country, and bringing us all together was just too expensive. But my hunger to get back to music was stimulated by the few shows we did do, and I started to feel more of a need to get going again with every passing day.

Since early in 2012, after resisting the suggestions of numerous friends for quite a while, I began working on writing my memoir. That kept me busy for over two years, and for the first number of months, it was enough to dominate my time and energy. When I finally finished, I found I had too lengthy a manuscript to be marketed. But long before then, I had started getting those musical urges again. Those urges were briefly tamped down by the Boulder County Conspiracy thing, but as I said, that didn't last long. In the end, it only stimulated my yearnings to try it again.

Then, in September of 2013, a wonderful thing happened. One day when Mary and I were in the supermarket, we ran into Milt Muth, an old friend who had just moved back to town. He had been in Cleveland with his father, who was nearing the end of his life.

When Milt's dad passed away, he came back to Colorado. Milt was a really good bass guitarist who I had talked with about forming a group a few years before I had my injury, but nothing had ever come of the plan.

When we met that day, the first thing Milt asked was whether I was still interested in pursuing anything like forming a band. Two weeks earlier I wouldn't have been interested. But due to a strange turn of events that had taken place a few days prior, Milt had caught me at the perfect time. I asked him what he had in mind.

He said that he had already renewed his musical relationship with Michael Reese, a wonderful guitarist who had quite a sparkling reputation in Colorado music circles. After a few phone calls and some idea exchanges, the three of us set about putting a new group together. It took some time, but eventually we found Andy Sweetser to cover the drums and Bob Schlesinger to play keyboards. We knew we still needed another strong voice to complete our sound since none of the other guys were first-class singers.

Then Jim Mason, Firefall's original producer, moved back out to Colorado from Florida and brought Jim Brady with him. Jim was a guitarist and lead singer in his own right, and filled the bill nicely. We decided to call ourselves Rick Roberts and Winter Rose. The name sounded good to us and served as a gentle reference to the fact that nobody in the band was in the early stages of their adulthood. And that in turn reminded us that the clock was ticking.

It was spring of 2014 before we got everyone lined up and hit the rehearsal grind.

I soon discovered that getting a band worked into shape is different when the people are in their fifties and sixties than it is when we were all in our twenties. At that earlier age, everybody can go all in and give the group their full attention. But usually there comes a point where the wiser among us realize that you can't spend your entire life chasing a dream.

In an older age group, most of the guys have families, jobs, bills, and various other responsibilities. With those restrictions, it was slow going to get things in motion. If we managed to squeeze in three rehearsals in a week, we felt like we had been functioning at breakneck speed. Most weeks we were able to coordinate two practices with the whole band, and a third dedicated to vocal rehearsal. We included Jim Mason to give us arrangement assistance and whatever other pointers occurred to him.

For me, one of the most challenging aspects of the job was trying to teach the band certain little nuances I had in my songs without having the ability to just sit down and demonstrate them on the guitar. In over forty years of music, I had always been able to use my instrument to show everyone what was supposed to be happening, so it was weird to have to just try and tell people what I wanted to hear and how to play it. I also have to say that standing there in rehearsal without an instrument was pretty strange, too. I've never claimed to be a threat to Mick Jagger, and it's a good thing I haven't, because standing there with nothing but a mike stand showed anybody who was watching that I was not up there to wow them with my cool moves.

I'd be lying if I didn't acknowledge the residual effects of my injury on my stage dancing abilities, but it wouldn't be fair to focus too much on performing as the crisis time. The truth is, that's one thing I haven't recovered—my dancing skills, even off stage. I was never Fred Astaire, but I can never remember *embarrassing* myself on the dance floor. These days, if I try to cut a rug (age giveaway) at all, I tend to mostly use my upper body. I don't feel stable enough if I move my feet around too much. So I kind of shuffle. But Mary doesn't mind at all. She just dances around me.

The Home Stretch

Chapter Twenty-Three

Now we're getting around to what's happened in my life since I finished the hands-on, day-to-day work of my recovery (or recoveries).

First, the easy stuff. As I said earlier, once I put down the bottle, I left it down. As of November 2015, I'll be celebrating eight years of sobriety, and I still don't miss it. But I'd like to take this opportunity to make a last statement about drinking.

There was, and is, no question that I am an alcoholic, so when I talk about how at the end of my drinking days, boredom was the main driving factor, it may seem a bit confusing, or as if I am trying to make my drinking sound like something else than what it was. I'm not. I will say it again. I *am* an alcoholic. And I believe and accept that alcoholism is a disease.

But I also believe something else. I believe that ultimately, stopping a drinking habit is a matter of choice. You simply have to come to a point in your own mind where you no longer *want* to drink. I don't mean that what you have to do is not allow yourself to drink or be able to fight off the cravings every minute of every day. No, I don't mean the point where you do not want to drink. I mean the point where what you *want* is *not* to drink. I mean you have to have an active *desire* not to drink. There can be any number of reasons to make your lust for alcohol fade away.

Mine was boredom for starters, but that was only one factor in my decision. My health was a consideration, but obviously that alone was not enough to make the change in my behavior. Besides the fact that I no longer got the same feeling from it, at some point I realized I had never really liked the way it tasted anyway. I completely agree with the fact that many people are predisposed to the addiction by virtue of genetics. But I think that even those folks are capable of beating the habit if they want to badly enough. I know that some people are going to disagree with me and say that certain individuals among us just don't have a choice. They'll claim it's that fact which qualifies it as a disease. But I stand my ground. I think that ultimately, you've got to make a choice. And the

Lame Brain

ability to make that choice is available to everyone, genetics or not.

Don't be misled by my saying that everyone can make their own choice. Making your own choice to quit is one thing. *Doing it on your own* is something else again. It's not as if someone can just decide that they're done with the bottle and that will be the end of it. Many, if not most people, will need every bit of help they can get. That's what Alcoholics Anonymous is all about. One of the biggest benefits of that organization is to consistently and continually remind the alcoholic that he or she is not alone and needn't be ashamed of his or her condition. The exposure to and fellowship of others who are also trying to change their habits is a great source of strength. And just as important is the emotional support of those who love you.

I will say one other thing regarding that choice. For some, it's really no harder than focusing on what's really going on. Getting serious about their lives and facing reality. For those people, it's really not that hard. They just need to pull off the blinders and face the truth of the situation.

For others, making that choice will make any other decision in their lives seem about as important as choosing which shirt to wear on a certain day. Letting go of their habit will be gut-wrenchingly difficult. They will have to completely reorder their priorities and look at the most dramatic question of all. Do they want to live, or would they rather die? Because that's the *real* issue for an alcoholic.

When I found out my health was suffering more than I had known, it was just the icing on the cake. Window dressing, if you will. That might sound strange, but my medical issues just provided me with an excuse to stop. I can't speak for anyone else, because I've seen too many friends who were given ample evidence of why they *had* to stop drinking, and still didn't.

But that doesn't negate what I'm saying about losing your desire to drink. Those friends of mine were just never able to find something else they wanted more than they wanted booze. So they chose the booze. And whether consciously or not, by choosing as they did, they answered the question of whether they would rather live or die by choosing the latter.

Needing to not drink is not the same as *wanting not to drink*. No matter what you need, if you still *want* to drink, you eventually will. It's all in the attitude and what it is you really *want* to do.

I think there are much healthier reasons than getting bored with it to lose your desire. Probably the best one is finding something else you like to do better. Giving up the habit for someone you love works pretty well. I've heard a lot of people say that love has never been enough to pull them away from the bottle, even though they claimed that some other thing or person was their greatest love. I once said that about myself, and I got set straight in a big hurry. The conversation was with my doctor, and it went like this:

Me: *"I love Mary more than anything in the world, and I know my drinking* hurts her, so I do my best to keep her from being exposed to it."

(Dr.) David Luce: *"You're a liar."*

Me: *"What? What do you mean?"*

David: *"You don't love Mary more than anything. You love your bottle more. If you loved her more, you'd stop your drinking."*

Now that may sound like he was telling me that if I loved her more, I would no longer *allow* myself to drink. But that was not what he was saying. He was making the statement that if I truly loved her more than my booze, I would lose the desire to do something that I knew caused her pain. In my very heart. And in the end, that was the biggest reason why I lost my desire to drink.

Please don't confuse losing the desire to drink with acquiring an active desire *not* to drink. At that point, I hadn't yet learned the difference between the two. So it was still a while before it all came together and I quit.

There was quite a lengthy span of time when I didn't care one way or the other whether I had a drink or not. But with nothing better to do, I saw no reason *not* to. I may have had nothing for it, but I had nothing against it either. That state of mind continued until I finally decided (with the help of the medical information I had been given) that I really did have some measurable negative feelings about my habit, and that's when I made my move.

And my situation was a little more complicated than that. I not only was (and still am) an alcoholic, but separate from that, I had a drinking habit. It's not necessary to be an alcoholic to have a drinking habit. I know a number of people in that category.

When I talk about a drinking habit, I'm referring to people who are just in the habit of drinking, the same way some people are in the habit of taking their shower before breakfast. It is simply a pattern of behavior that they get used to and eventually becomes standard operating procedure. That doesn't automatically qualify them as an alcoholic. It just tags them as predictable. Some can walk away from liquor as easily as any other *habit* because they are not addicted so much as they are lacking in discipline.

It's also not required to have a drinking habit to be an alcoholic. I have seen people whose drinking follows no particular pattern at all. Like binge drinkers. They may stay clean for weeks or months, but they will invariably return to the bottle sooner or later until they finally make that sincere and serious decision to stop. And when they do drink, they usually aren't moderate about it. I don't consider those people to have a habit because they are totally unpredictable and have no pattern to their consumption. But they do have an addiction. And strangely enough, those people (the bingers) are usually the last to see or admit their problem simply *because* they don't drink all the time. They're also, coincidentally, the ones in the most danger of some traumatic alcohol death from a binge that goes too far and results in acute and fatal alcohol poisoning.

What I'm trying to say about the habit and the addiction is that they are separate things and not *necessarily* mutually inclusive. But I had both, so I not only had to confront my addiction, I also had to break a bad habit. With my health at issue as a reasonable motivator, and my sense of boredom in play, I finally decided to put down the bottle (*and* broke the habit) in November of 2007.

I do have a plan "B" now that I've had a few years to think about it. Since my abstention from liquor is based on that being the way I want it and not something I am denying myself, I have never been troubled by cravings or alcohol dreams. I talked about that one dream of humiliating myself at a concert, which I used to have while I was still boozing. I had that one too many times.

It felt the same as those dreams most of us had as kids where you're walking down the street in your own neighborhood completely naked and there's nowhere to hide, and you're moving in slow motion. Extremely unpleasant. Or maybe I'm the only one who had that dream.

Anyhow, like I said, I have a plan "B". My plan is if I ever find that I'm having cravings, I will drive directly to the nearest liquor store and go to the door. Then I will stop and ask myself a single one-word question. That question will be *"Why?"*

If I can find a satisfactory answer to that question, I will go in and buy myself a fifth of tequila. But I don't think I'm in too much danger of that happening.

So to sum it all up, there is one suggestion I would like to offer to those who are having trouble with drinking and would honestly and wholeheartedly like to break the habit. I believe that anyone, and I mean *anyone,* can break away from alcohol if they truly want to. It may involve rehab. It might take more than one attempt. It will most likely be assisted by Alcoholics Anonymous or some other strong support system. And it will certainly require something or someone you value more than booze. Something to occupy your mind, your body, your heart, and your time. But the choice will ultimately be up to you. It's never too late to break the cycle if you really want to. Always remember the liver is the only organ that can regenerate itself, so the only point of no return is when you have completely destroyed that organ. Only a few people take it that far without having already made their decision of whether to live or die. It's hard to reach that point in the process and still be taken by surprise. If you want to live, don't ever give up. *You CAN do it!*

* * *

Now that I've said my piece about alcohol, there are a few other areas of my life that are still going forward.

On the music and performance front, things are proceeding at their own pace. After Rick Roberts and Winter Rose did their debut performance, some questions were raised about whether my voice was up to the task. Jim Mason,

Firefall's old producer, brought up the issue first, and when I talked to the band members they expressed a bit of concern too, although not as much as Jim had.

I've long since accepted that my voice is not the same one I had when I was twenty-five years old, in part as a result of my injury, partially from taking fifteen years off, and partially because of forty years of time slipping by. But I firmly believe I can still sing very well, and that I am quite capable of fronting a group at any level. I knew the changes my voice had undergone didn't have to be a game-breaker if I was willing to be flexible and realistic. My first responsibility should always be to make sure the men I work with are comfortable up there on stage with me.

When people think of singing, they don't always perceive the voice as an instrument, but that's just what it is. And mine has changed some. With that in mind, I had to come to terms with the idea that I was now going to have to learn how to play my new instrument. So I got myself into training. I hired two vocal instructors and started switching off on alternate weeks with them. They've both helped me learn how to use my voice correctly and do the things I had never paid attention to before. I'm amazed I got away without using any proper technique for as long as I did. Simple things like knowing how to breathe properly can make a world of difference. I won't go into the many things I've learned, but my instructors and I are really pleased with the results.

Eventually I cut back to using just one instructor so I could focus on a particular approach to improving my singing. As of this writing, I am still working with her and continuing to learn more techniques and methods to get the very most out of my pipes.

Coincidentally, the band had to take a hiatus because our manager hit a span of serious health issues, and because we needed to make a personnel change. As a result of some hard lessons I learned in earlier musical endeavors, trying to chart a course in music without strong and steady direction was not something I was willing to do *again*. Without someone outside the band in charge to help the group make the right decisions, it's a good bet the band will choose wrong five times as often as they get things right.

During the "vacation" we took so I could polish up my voice and the manager could polish up his health, I had time to look closely at how we could make the group even better. I figured out that we were missing a strong voice capable of singing above me. And, as fate would have it, Jim Brady went back to Florida, so we would have had to replace him anyway. At present, I have two likely and very talented possible candidates to fill the gap. So the timing worked out fairly well and it looks like we'll be back on track very soon. Once we have everything up to speed, I have high hopes and expectations about what we'll be able to accomplish with our music.

* * *

Lame Brain

The biggest thing is what has happened as far as my brain injury. I can only say that I thank the Lord every night for his generosity to me in so many ways, but ranking right up at the top is the nearly complete recovery He has provided for me. I won't rehash what I've already said about my feelings that my recovery was a joint effort between heaven and me, and how I expected myself to take care of the day-to-day heavy lifting, but I ain't discounting the Lord's involvement in the equation, either.

Occasionally I wonder if all the injuries and scrape ups I spoke about in Chapter One were just my personal spring training for the main event that took place in May of 2006.

You may recall that way back in Chapter Two that I asked a couple of questions about my injury when it finally manifested itself a month after the actual fall. I wanted to know why only my legs were put out of commission and why it took so long before the unhappy effects kicked in. I guess I wasn't too curious at the time because I never bothered to follow up with the doctors so I could get the answers to my questions. It wasn't until I started writing this book that I actually went in search of the information I needed.

I got the medical records from the emergency room, and found out some things that surprised me. The first one was minor. All these years I've had the date of my hospital visit set as Mother's Day, May 12th, 2006. I found that I was actually admitted to the ER on Mother's Day, May 14th, 2006. No biggie. But...I've always thought I spent a few hours there and then went home. The records say otherwise. According to official hospital documents, I was admitted to the hospital and spent two days there. It makes me wonder whether my memory of when the doctor informed me I was going to stop moving under my own power came in the ER, or closer to my discharge. Not that the timing of his diagnosis matters in and of itself; he still made the prediction weeks before the event.

But in terms of actual answers, the records don't tell the story. There's not a word about any projected effects from the injury, although there are several references to no foreseeable physical consequences.

The general opinion about why only my legs were affected has to do with the placement of the hematoma in my brain. In all honesty, I don't remember whether anyone ever said that only my legs would stop working. Nor did anyone tell me I'd lose more than that. I don't think anything was ever said one way or the other. It was probably just my curiosity about why my loss should be so localized. That's not including the reduced skills of my right arm, but that's not really the same, because I can do almost every other thing I could before with that arm. And with practice, I'll think I'll be able to work those skills out, too. At least I'm not going to stop trying.

I then made an effort to find out if the attending physician might have any recollection of how he came to his conclusion of my impending loss. When

I tracked him down, he couldn't remember my case well enough, nor did the records reveal to him how he was able to foresee my medical future. He theorized that the time element may also have had to do with the placement of the damage, but we didn't have any X-rays to look at, so he was reluctant to say anything definite.

So I still haven't been able to find out for certain why my legs suffered no immediate dysfunction. And even back when I was being treated, the doctor had been unwilling to say *when* it would happen; he just promised it would be sometime soon.

Maybe somewhere out there in the world is a medical man who could tell me exactly how my doctor knew those things. I confess I really didn't look into the matter that diligently because in the end it really isn't that important *how* my doctor knew. What is important is that he *did* know, and that he let me know it didn't have to be permanent.

Overall, I guess that's the only thing that counts. For all intents and purposes, my injury and the whole ordeal is a piece of the past that taught me a number of unexpected but significant lessons that were only peripherally related to my campaign to walk again. Patience, persistence, the overwhelming necessity of never giving up, even when things seemed hopeless, and a hundred other things I hadn't needed to think about before were suddenly of the utmost importance if I planned to stay in the fight. Those are things I hope I never forget, and things I have already found very useful in other areas of my life.

I still can't get my right arm to cooperate when I try any complicated strumming patterns, and my balance is not the thing of beauty it once was, but I can walk fine, and there are no other obvious impairments beyond those of any sixty-five year old man. And my friends tell me I don't look a day over sixty-four and a half!

In the final reckoning, I'm having a wonderful time walking, singing, and staying sober. There are a whole lot of exciting things I still plan to do in this life I've been given another shot at, so stay tuned, because IT AIN'T OVER YET!

Epilogue

By Mary Roberts

I can't say enough about the challenge it is for people who are trying to recover, either from injury or addiction. One statement comes to my mind: don't ever give up!

When Rick got hurt, as a spouse and a caregiver, my total vision was to focus on each day and try to stay in the moment. When the injury occurred, it came out of the blue. I knew I needed to surround myself with positive people, positive environments, and a lot of love. I remember calling my family and sharing the news. I cried, and I cried hard! My eyes were so swollen I could hardly see. It was like the injury had happened to me, only triple-fold.

The first questions that came to my mind? Where could I turn for support and who could I really trust? Will I *by myself* be able to recover from this? I felt so broken in so many ways. But I was fortunate to have the help of professionals and the love and support of our families and close friends.

And it wouldn't be fair if I didn't mention the help that was provided to me by Bingo, our Golden Retriever assistance dog, and Maggie, the other canine member of the family. Their unconditional love was so much of a boost, not only to me, but to Rick, too.

I will be eternally grateful to the employers who helped me structure my working schedule in a way that allowed me to be there for Rick as much as possible.

When things of this magnitude happen, remember that every day we are on this earth is a true blessing. And you have to be patient. Getting your body and your mind back to full speed often takes years. You have to take it one day at a time. And you'll have to realize when you need to regain your health, it's not only physically, but an emotional and financial challenge, too.

When we finally found the right therapist and he saw the condition Rick was in, his first statement to me was "Take my hand, and let's go on a special journey together." He introduced us to his team, and I could see how they were filled with real heart and pride. In the first session, Rick was put on a walker with a gate belt, and he managed to walk four steps. At that point, I knew we had started our journey. During the span of our efforts, they helped immensely with the healing process.

I'm now thirty years sober myself, so when Rick first entered my life, it was easy to see he had alcohol issues. But having been down that road myself, I knew that those issues weren't going to just disappear overnight. I also knew that ultimately, only he could make the choices necessary to end his use of liquor, so with this situation, too, I was going to have to exercise a lot of patience. What I *could* do was offer an unspoken request that he take an honest look at what he was doing to himself. And the strongest medicine I had to offer was my ongoing, unconditional love.

If you have someone in your life that needs your support, don't give up on them. I never gave up on Rick and I'm so glad I didn't. We have been happily married for over twenty-two years and every day with him has been a blessing for me.

Dear Reader,

TBI is a serious subject. Notwithstanding my rather off hand way of discussing the topic, it has not been my intent to make light of brain injuries, but to help people think and take the subject more seriously. Please let me know what you think by putting a review on the site where you purchased the book, or sending me an email through my website, rickrobertsmusic.com. I love to hear from my friends (and I consider you all my friends)!

Rick Roberts

P.S. And no matter what life brings your way, just remember it'll be alright.

About the Author

Rick Roberts is a 40-year veteran of the rock'n'roll wars. He began his recording career in 1970 with the Flying Burrito Brothers and was a major contributor to their last two albums. He went on to do two solo albums and then form the well-known band Firefall in 1974, with whom he played for seven years during their heyday. He has also been a member of Stephen Stills' band and Linda Ronstadt's band during his career, and has been awarded two platinum and four gold albums for his efforts. He has had over 60 of his compositions recorded and performed by such artists as The Burritos, Firefall, Stephen Stills, Linda Ronstadt, Barry Manilow, The Dirt Band, and numerous others. He is the composer of the hit songs "Just Remember I Love You", "You Are The Woman", "Strange Way", "Colorado", and several more that graced the Top 40 at one time or another. His compositions have over 13 million airplays worldwide.

After suffering a debilitating brain injury in 2006 which left him in jeopardy of never walking again, it took him nearly four years of intense physical therapy to walk again without crutches or other aids. Rick currently lives and works in Longmont, Colorado with his wife, Mary, and their two dogs (Donovan and Maggie) and two cats (Bean and Minky). Rick is currently playing with his new band, Rick Roberts And Winter Rose. Visit Rick on his website at: www.rickrobertsmusic.com.

www.ingramcontent.com/pod-product-compliance
Lightning Source LLC
Chambersburg PA
CBHW060531100426
42743CB00009B/1486